FTM 2017

Companion Guide

to

Family Tree Maker®

Based on the original Companion Guide by

Tana L. Pedersen

2103-6-01

Contents

Part 4: Managing Your Trees

Chapter 12 Working with Trees

Introduction

Congratulations on selecting Family Tree Maker to discover and preserve your family's heritage. It's easy to use for those just starting to research their family history, but it's also powerful enough for the most serious genealogist. Use Family Tree Maker to store, display, and share any kind of family information—from names, marriages, and deaths to priceless family stories, photos, and videos.

This guide is designed to help you learn Family Tree Maker quickly, leaving you more time to discover your family history. Even if you have never used a genealogy program before, you'll find that the features in Family Tree Maker make it possible to keep track of even the most tangled of family trees.

This book is written with the novice computer user in mind. You'll read about many of the useful tools that the casual Family Tree Maker user never discovers, and you'll be taken on a hands-on trip through the program. The many illustrations let you check your progress as you master each new feature or concept. Even if you are familiar with computers, though, you may have only recently been introduced to Family Tree Maker or simply want to know what great features you have not yet discovered in the program. This book offers you a step-by-step tour of the program and all that you can accomplish with it.

Before you begin entering your family's information, be sure to check out the "Family Tree Maker Basics" chapter. It will give you the skills you need to navigate through Family Tree Maker and will familiarize you with the software's interface.

What's New?

New features and enhancements in Family Tree Maker 2017 make it easier than ever to discover your family history, build your family tree, and share your unique heritage. Here are four of the most notable new features you will find as you explore Family Tree Maker 2017:

 FamilySearch Integration. Family Tree Maker users can now directly access online records of FamilySearch, the world's largest collection of genealogical and historical records, much like they already do with Ancestry.com. Users can search more than a billion names in FamilySearch's Family Tree database, get match suggestions (hints), and merge the results into their trees. See pages 125-137.

 FamilySync™. An upgrade from Ancestry's TreeSync® technology, FamilySync™ allows Family Tree Maker 2017 users to synchronize the trees on their computer with Ancestry trees, as well as to simply upload their trees to and download their trees from Ancestry. Those using both a desktop and laptop computer will appreciate the new ability to sync both to a single Ancestry tree online. See pages 238-246.

 Color Coding. Providing the ability to mark up to eight colors at a time on a single person, color coding helps users organize their records and gain helpful insights into their family's unique history. Together with sophisticated filter tools, color coding allows users to uncover crossed family lines and identify relationships that might otherwise have never been discovered. See pages 51-53.

Photo Darkroom™. Photo Darkroom provides elegantly simple but powerful photo editing tools designed specifically for genealogists. The first set of tools, a photo repair suite, makes it possible to take old black-and-white photographs faded beyond recognition and, in just a few clicks, restore them to look almost like the day they were printed. See pages 98-99.

How the Guide Is Organized

As you read this book, you'll notice several features that provide you with useful information:

- Tips give you advice on the best ways to perform tasks.

- Notes offer you timely hints and explanations about how features work.

- Sidebars give you additional information on a variety of family history topics, such as using maps, that will enhance your ability to create a richer and more complete family tree.

- A glossary explains words you might not be familiar with, such as Family Tree Maker terms (family group view, Fastfields), and genealogy terms (GEDCOM, Ahnentafel).

If you still need help, a quick perusal of the Table of Contents should lead you right to the task you are trying to perform; if not, check the index in the back of the book.

Part One
Getting Started

Chapter One
Installing Family Tree Maker

This chapter lists the system requirements for Family Tree Maker, shows you how to install the software, and gives a quick introduction to available help resources.

Recommended System Requirements

To use Family Tree Maker, you'll need a computer that meets the specifications below. Keep in mind that the more information in your tree, the greater the amount of free hard drive space and available RAM you will need. If you have lots of images or videos, you'll need a substantial amount of hard drive space.

- Operating system: Microsoft Windows® 7 or later, including Windows® 10

- Hard disk space: 900 MB for installation

- Memory: 2 GB RAM minimum (4 GB recommended)

- Display: 1024x768 resolution monitor

- DVD drive (only if installing from a DVD)

All online features require Internet access. The user is responsible for their Internet Service Provider (ISP) account, all Internet access fees, and phone charges.

Installing Family Tree Maker

To use Family Tree Maker the software must be installed on your computer's hard drive; you cannot run it directly from the DVD or the USB drive. If you have an earlier version of Family Tree Maker installed on your computer, this new version will not copy over it. While the installation process will not harm your existing Family Tree Maker files, it's always a good idea to back up your tree files on an external storage device or using a cloud storage service.

1. Insert the Family Tree Maker DVD, or double-click the .exe file that you have downloaded or that is located on your Family Tree Maker USB Drive.

2. Run the Family Tree Maker installer.

3. On the Welcome screen, click Next to continue, and then follow the onscreen instructions.

    Note: If you experience any difficulties, please see the "Installation Problems" section of the "Troubleshooting" chapter on page 302.

Registering the Software

Before you create your first tree, take a minute to register the software. Registered users get discounts on new editions of Family Tree Maker and notifications of software updates.

When you open the application for the first time, the registration dialog opens automatically. If you choose not to register on the first run, but decide to do so some time later, select **Register Family Tree Maker** from the **Help** menu, and then follow the onscreen instructions. Make sure your computer is connected to the Internet before you start.

License Agreement

Please read the license agreement. You can view it during the software installation or at a later time. The *License* text file is located in the same folder on your hard drive where you installed Family Tree Maker.

Getting Help

Family Tree Maker has a built-in Help system, this companion guide, and online technical support. If you have questions about a feature or simply want to learn more about the program, check out one of these resources.

Help Program

To access Help, go to the **Help** menu and select **Help for Family Tree Maker**; or press the **F1** key. Use these tabs on the Help window (fig. 1-1) to find the topic you're interested in:

- **Contents tab.** Click to view topics arranged in chapters, like a book's table of contents.

- **Index tab.** Click to view topics by words and phrases.

- **Search tab.** Click to look for specific words or phrases within Help topics. Many useful topic pages can be found by entering keywords such as "adding," "creating," and "merging."

Navigating in the Help Program

The Help program uses blue, underlined links to take you to related topics. Simply click any link to go to a new topic. Use these options to move around within the Help program:

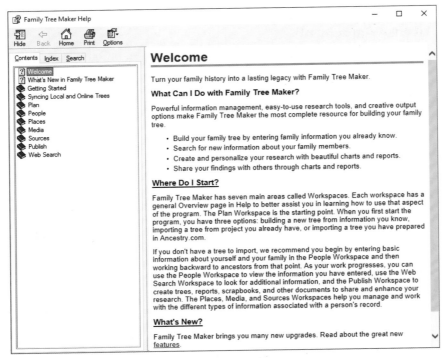

Figure 1-1. The Welcome window in the Help program.

- **Hide/Show.** Click to show and hide the tab view of the Help window.

- **Back.** Click to return to Help pages you've viewed already.

- **Home.** Click to return to the Welcome window.

- **Print.** Click to print the currently selected Help page.

- **Options button.** Click to display a sub-menu of additional options, such as "Search Highlight On," which you can use to highlight search terms on a Help page.

Tooltips

If you want to know the name of a button or find out what it's used for, hold the pointer over it for a second or two and a tooltip will appear.

Companion Guide

To view this *Companion Guide* as a PDF, select **Companion Guide** from the **Help** menu. (If you are unable to open the PDF, you may need to install Adobe Reader, which is available as a free download from the Adobe website at www.adobe.com.)

Technical Support

Family Tree Maker has an online help center, where you can get help for technical problems and answers to customer service questions. You'll also find easy-to-understand articles, tips, and step-by-step instructions. Choose **Family Tree Maker Tech Support** from the **Help** menu.

Feedback

We'd love to hear from you with comments, questions or suggestions. Please visit the Family Tree Maker product page online. Choose **Provide Family Tree Maker Feedback** from the **Help** menu, or go to www.familytreemaker.com, and then use one of the feedback options available there.

Chapter Two
Family Tree Maker Basics

Family Tree Maker makes it easy—and enjoyable—for anyone to discover their family history and gather it into one convenient location. And whether you're interested in printing family charts to share at a reunion or looking for an easy way to store your family facts, photos, and records, Family Tree Maker is the program to help you do it all.

This chapter gives you the basic skills and knowledge you need to launch the program and navigate around the software. Let's get started.

Opening and Closing Family Tree Maker

To open the program, double-click the **Family Tree Maker 2017** icon on your computer desktop or click the Windows **Start** button and select **Family Tree Maker 2017**.

To close the program, click **File > Exit** or click the **Close** button (**X**) in the upper-right corner. There's no need to save your tree— Family Tree Maker automatically saves changes as you make them.

The Family Tree Maker Interface

To use any computer program effectively, the first step is to understand its unique interface and tools. You'll immediately recognize many common features in Family Tree Maker. However, there are some toolbars, menus, and windows you'll want to learn how to use.

Toolbars

The main toolbar in Family Tree Maker (fig. 2-1) is located at the top of the window above the menu bar. It provides quick navigation to various workspaces—groupings of the most important features in the software. On the far left of the toolbar, you'll find the Select Tree drop-down list that lets you switch between trees.

Figure 2-1. The main toolbar.

Menus and Keyboard Shortcuts

Family Tree Maker menus work like in any other computer program. Simply click a menu name to display its options; then, click the option you want. Some menu options have keyboard shortcuts that allow you to access features without using a mouse or trackpad.

Workspaces Overview

Family Tree Maker groups important features together in workspaces. Each workspace has a slightly different appearance and purpose, but generally, they all contain the same elements, such as toolbars and tabs.

The Plan Workspace

The Plan workspace is the "control center" where you manage your family trees. On the New Tree tab you can start a new tree, import an existing tree file, or download a tree from Ancestry.

Figure 2-2. The Current Tree tab on the Plan workspace.

The Current Tree tab on the Plan workspace (fig. 2-2) lets you view details about your tree, manage your research to-do list, and, if you've linked your desktop tree to an online tree, you can also manage how the trees are synced. The Current Tree tab also contains the Ancestry Web Dashboard where you can see the status of your Ancestry subscription if you have one (double-click it to access your Ancestry account), open your Ancestry trees, and view your Member Connect activity.

What Is Member Connect on Ancestry?

Member Connect helps you stay in touch with others who are researching your ancestors. Ancestry scans public Ancestry trees and notifies you when there's activity around records you've saved or commented on.

The People Workspace

The People workspace is where you enter information about individuals and families in your tree—and where you will spend most of your time in Family Tree Maker.

The Tree tab (fig. 2-3) provides a comprehensive view of your family. You can see several generations of your family at once and easily navigate to each person in your tree. Because you will use this tab often, its various sections are explained in detail.

Figure 2-3. The Tree tab on the People workspace.

The Index

The Index (fig. 2-4) lists all the individuals in your tree and is one of the easiest ways to locate the person you want to focus on. To view information for a specific individual, simply click his or her name in the Index. If you can't see the person you want, use the scroll bar to move up and down the list, or type a name in the Find field to jump to a particular person.

The house icon indicates the individual who is the current home person in the tree. (You'll learn more about the home person in chapter 3.)

To make it easier to locate individuals, you can change how the Index sorts names using the **Sort** drop-down list. Also, you can add birth, marriage, or death dates by clicking the **Show additional data in index** button.

You can also limit the Index so it displays only certain individuals; click the **Filter** button and choose a specific family line, an individual's descendants, or a group of your choice. Click the **Bookmarks** button to see a list of individuals you have specifically bookmarked, or click the **History** button to see the individuals you have added or edited recently.

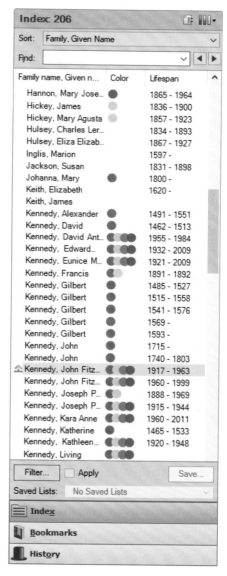

Figure 2-4. The Index.

Saving and Opening Filtered Lists of People

When you have applied a filter, you may want to retain the list of people that it produced so that you can return to it whenever you need. You can save the list by clicking the **Save** button at the bottom of the **Index**. In the dialog that appears, give the list a name and click **Save**. You can also choose a color. This color will be assigned to all the people in the list and displayed next to their names in the Index and on their thumbnails in the tree viewer, exactly as colors assigned with color coding are. For more information about color coding, see the "Color Coding" section on page 51.

Figure 2-5. The Save List dialog.

When you save your list, it appears in the **Saved Lists** drop-down list below the **Save** button. To open a saved list, click the drop-down list and choose the list you want.

Managing Saved Lists

- To manage lists, choose **Manage Lists** from the **Saved Lists** drop-down list.

- To add a new list, either save an existing one (see "Saving and Opening Filtered Lists of People" above) or click the "plus" button in the Manage Lists dialog. The **Filter Individuals** dialog appears. Set up a filter to produce the list you need, and then click **Apply**. In the dialog that appears, give the list a name and, optionally, choose a color, and then click **OK**.

- To delete an existing list, select its name in the **Manage Lists** dialog, and then click the "minus" button.

- To change a list's name or color, select the list in the **Manage Lists** dialog, and then edit the name in the **Name** field or click a different color.

The Tree Viewer

The tree viewer (fig. 2-6) helps you navigate your family tree as well as enter new individuals.

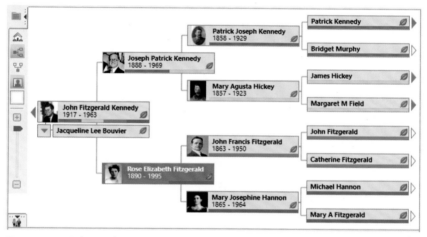

Figure 2-6. The pedigree view in the tree viewer.

These buttons will help you use the tree viewer:

 Go to home person. Makes the home person the primary individual or focus of the tree.

 Pedigree view. Shows a pedigree view of your tree. The primary individual or focus of the tree is on the left, with ancestors branching out to the right.

 Family view. Shows a family view of your tree. The primary individual is at the base of the tree, with ancestors branching above—paternal on the left and maternal on the right.

Include pictures. Displays portraits and lifespans for each individual in the pedigree view.

 Re-center on selected person. Adjusts the tree to focus on the currently selected person in the family view.

 Background color. Lets you choose the tree viewer's background color.

The Editing Panel

The editing panel (fig. 2-7) is where you'll enter basic information about an individual, such as birth, marriage, and death dates and places. At the top you'll find a portrait of an individual (if you've added one) and how he or she is related to the home person. Toolbar buttons under the portrait let you display media items, notes, Web links, and tasks associated with the individual.

Figure 2-7. The editing panel.

The Family Group View

The family group view (fig. 2-8) lets you view an individual's spouse and children.

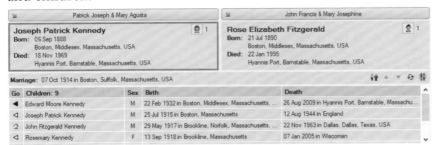

Figure 2-8. The family group view on the People workspace.

Click the "parents" button above the individual to display his or her parents and siblings. The toolbar buttons let you edit the couple's marriage fact, change the display order of their children, and view blended families.

The Person Tab

The Person tab on the People workspace (fig. 2-9) lets you add facts, media items, Web links, and notes for an individual. You can also view a timeline for an individual and their relationships to other family members.

Figure 2-9. The Person tab on the People workspace.

The Places Workspace

The Places workspace (fig. 2-10) helps you view the locations you've entered for events—and gives you the opportunity to view online maps of them. The Places panel on the left shows every location you've entered in your tree. When you click on a place, it will be displayed in the map at the center of the workspace. The details panel on the right side shows the individuals who have life events associated with the location.

Figure 2-10. The Places workspace.

The Media Workspace

The Media workspace acts as a storage space for your photos, audio recordings, movies, family documents, and historical records. On the Collection tab (fig. 2-11) you can view thumbnails of your media items and enter information about them. On the Detail tab you can add notes for an item and link it to individuals and source citations.

Figure 2-11. The Collection tab on the Media workspace.

The Sources Workspace

The Sources workspace (fig. 2-12) organizes your sources and source citations. The Source Groups panel on the left lets you sort sources by person, title, and repository; the sources display area shows which citations have been entered for a specific source. Tabs at the bottom of the window show the individuals linked to a source citation, related notes, and media items. In the editing panel, you can enter or update specific source citations.

Figure 2-12. The Sources workspace.

The Publish Workspace

The Publish workspace offers a variety of charts and reports that you can view, print, and share. You can also create family history books. The Collection tab (fig. 2-13) shows the types of charts and reports that are available and gives an explanation of each.

On the Detail tab you can customize a chart or report using the editing panel and preview your changes.

Figure 2-13. The Collection tab on the Publish workspace.

The Web Search Workspace

The Web Search workspace (fig. 2-14) lets you search billions of records on Ancestry and FamilySearch to find more information about your relatives—all without leaving Family Tree Maker. You can also search other websites and easily download discoveries into your tree.

Figure 2-14. The Web Search workspace.

Chapter Three
Creating a Tree

Before You Begin

This chapter assumes that you have installed Family Tree Maker and read chapters 1 and 2. Once you've learned a few of the basic Family Tree Maker features, you're ready to create your first tree. Make sure you have family information handy or have a file, such as a GEDCOM, or Ancestry tree to use.

Creating a Tree

A tree is where you gather and enter your family facts and details. If you've received a family history file from another family member or researcher, you can import the file, creating a new tree. Then you can begin adding your own information. You can also create a tree by entering a few quick facts about yourself or by downloading a tree you've created on Ancestry. Yet another way is to create a backup of an existing tree you have in Family Tree Maker 2017 on another computer and move it to the current computer. This allows you to keep two FTM trees (or more if you wish) and a linked Ancestry tree in sync. See "Working with Linked Trees" on page 238.

Entering Your Information from Scratch

If this is your first time creating a family tree, you'll want to use this option. Enter a few facts about yourself and your parents, and you're on your way.

1. Click the **Plan** button on the main toolbar to open the Plan workspace.

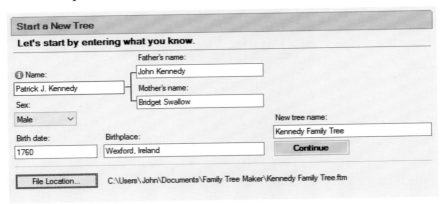

2. On the New Tree tab, click **Enter What You Know**.

3. Type your name and choose your gender. You can also enter your birth date and place and your parents' names.

4. Enter a name for the tree in the **New tree name** field.

5. By default, your tree file will be saved to a Family Tree Maker folder located in your documents folder. If you want to save the tree file to another folder, click **File Location**.

6. Click **Continue**. The tree opens on the People workspace, where you can start entering your family information.

How Many Trees Should You Create?

When most beginners create a family tree, their first question is, "Should I create one large, all-inclusive tree or several small trees, one for each family?" The truth is, there is no right answer.

The advantages to having one large tree are pretty clear. One computer file is easier to keep track of—one file to enter your information in, one file to back up, one file to share. Also, you won't have to duplicate your efforts by entering some data, sources, and media items in several trees.

Multiple trees can be useful too. The more trees you have, the smaller the tree files will typically be. If you have concerns about your computer's performance or have storage issues, smaller files might work best. Smaller tree files also make it easier to collaborate with other family members; you can send them only the family lines they're interested in.

Regardless of which way you organize your trees initially, don't feel like you're stuck with a permanent decision. The flexible nature of Family Tree Maker means you can merge files any time; you can even export parts of your tree to create a brand new tree.

Importing a Tree File

If you've already created a tree file or received one from another family member, you can import it. Tree files from previous versions of Family Tree Maker, GEDCOMs (GEnealogical Data COMmunications format), FamilySearch Personal Ancestral Files (PAFs), and *Legacy Family Tree* files are all compatible.

1. If you haven't already, copy the tree file you want to import to your computer's hard drive.

2. Click the **Plan** button on the main toolbar to open the Plan workspace.

3. On the New Tree tab, click **Import an Existing Tree**.

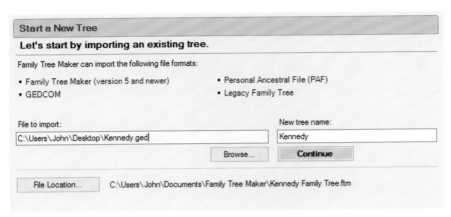

4. Click **Browse** to locate the tree file you want to import.

5. By default, your tree file will be saved to a Family Tree Maker folder located in your documents folder. If you want to save the tree file to another folder, click **File Location**.

6. If necessary, change the file's name in the **New tree name** field.

7. Click **Continue**. You'll see the Import Complete window, which shows statistics for the new tree, including the number of individuals, families, and sources that were imported.

8. Click **Close**. The tree opens on the People workspace, where you can start entering your family information.

Downloading a Tree from Ancestry

If you've created a tree on Ancestry, you don't need to start over in Family Tree Maker; you can download the tree to your computer. It will include all the facts, sources, and images you have attached to individuals.

Note: To download an Ancestry tree, you must be the tree's owner; you can't download trees you've been invited to view or edit.

Downloading and Linking a Tree in Family Tree Maker

When you download a tree from Ancestry, you create a link between your online Ancestry tree and its corresponding tree on your computer. This means that additions, deletions, or edits you make in your Family Tree Maker tree will be duplicated in your Ancestry tree (and vice versa). (For more information see "Differences Between FTM and Ancestry Trees" on page 236 and "Working with Linked Trees" on page 238.)

Note: When you download your Ancestry tree, a new FTM tree will be created and linked to your Ancestry tree. You can merge the new FTM tree with another FTM tree later if you wish, but not during the download.

1. Make sure you are logged in to your Ancestry account (if necessary click the **Log In** button in the upper-right corner of the Plan workspace).

2. Go to the New Tree tab on the Plan workspace and click **Download a Tree from Ancestry**. A list of your trees on Ancestry appears.

3. Select the tree that you want to download. A summary of the tree status appears to the right of the list of the trees.

4. Click the **Download Tree** button. The **Download an Ancestry Tree** dialog appears.

5. If you want to change the name of the tree, enter the new name in the **New FTM Tree** field.

6. Choose whether your Ancestry and FTM trees will be synced manually or automatically. (For help see "Setting Up Syncing" on page 239.)

7. Click the **Download Ancestry Citation Media** checkbox to also download all the Ancestry record images attached to your tree.

   Note: Ancestry Citation Media will not be downloaded unless you have a current paid Ancestry subscription. You can check your subscription status in the Web Dashboard. See page 11.

8. Click **Download**. When the tree has been downloaded successfully, click **Close**.

Creating a copy of an existing tree on another computer

If you already have a tree on Ancestry and on one of your computers, you can move a copy of it to a different computer on which Family Tree Maker 2017 is installed and keep all of the trees in sync. To do so, create a full backup of your existing FTM tree, copy it to your other computer using a flash drive, and then restore the tree there.

On the computer with the tree that you want to copy, do this:

1. In Family Tree Maker, open the tree that you want to copy.

2. Sync your tree with the Ancestry tree.

3. Choose **File** > **Backup**.

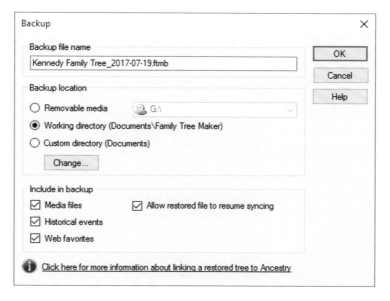

4. Select the checkboxes to include media files, historical events, and Web favorites in the backup.

5. Make sure that the **Allow restored file to resume syncing** checkbox is selected.

6. Choose a location on your computer to save the backup file.
    Note: If backing up directly to a flash drive fails with an error,
    try to backup to your computer and then copy the backup file to
    your flash drive.

7. Click **OK**.

Now copy the backup file onto your flash drive and then copy it
from the flash drive onto the other computer.

On the computer to which you have moved the backup file, do this:

1. Choose **File > Restore**.
2. Select the backup file and click **Open**.
3. Choose the location where you want Family Tree Maker to
    store your copied tree.
4. Click **Save**.
5. In the dialog that appears, make sure that the **Allow restored
    file to resume syncing** checkbox is selected, and then click **OK**.

Choosing a Home Person

Each tree has a home person. By default, this is the first person you
enter in a tree. If you're creating a tree based on your family, the
home person will most likely be you. However, the home person
can be anyone in your tree.

Occasionally, you may want to switch the home person. For
example, if you're working on a specific family line, you may want
to make someone in that ancestral line the home person.

Changing the Home Person on the Plan Workspace

1. Click the **Plan** button on the main toolbar and then click the **Current Tree** tab. At the top of the window, you'll see the name of the current home person.

2. Hover over "Home person" and click the button that appears.

3. In the Index of Individuals window, click the new home person and click **OK**.

Changing the Home Person on the People Workspace

1. Click the **People** button on the main toolbar; then click the **Tree** tab.

2. Find the appropriate person in the tree viewer or Index; then right-click the individual and click **Set As Home Person**.

Part Two
Building a Tree

Chapter Four
Entering Family Information

Much of your time using Family Tree Maker will be spent entering the names, dates, and events that you've uncovered about your family. The simplest way to build your tree is to begin with what you already know—basic details about yourself, your spouse, your children, and your parents. As your tree grows, your focus can turn to ancestral lines, such as your grandparents and great-grandparents.

When you've entered basic birth, marriage, and death information for your family, you can expand your tree by adding marriage details, immigration stories, medical histories, and more.

Entering Basic Information for an Individual

You can enter facts about an individual (such as birth and death dates) on the Tree tab in the People workspace.

1. Click the **People** button on the main toolbar to open the People workspace.

2. Click an individual's name in the Index or tree viewer. The person's name and gender will be displayed in the editing panel.

3. In the editing panel, enter a date in the **Birth** field.

4. Click the **Birth Place** field below and type the location where the individual was born.

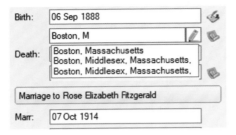

Tip: As you enter a location, you'll notice that a list of possible matches appears. To use a suggested location, click it; to ignore the suggestions, continue typing.

5. If you know an individual's death date and place, enter this too. You can now continue by adding marriage facts, entering additional family members, entering more facts for the individual, or adding photographs.

Entering Names

To keep names in your tree consistent, you'll want to follow these guidelines.

- Be sure to use a woman's maiden name (her last name before she was married). This helps you trace her family and keeps you from confusing her with other people in your tree.

- You may have last names (surnames) that are not a single word. You will need to identify these names with backslashes (\); otherwise, Family Tree Maker will read only the last word as the surname. Here are some examples:

    George \de la Vergne\   Teresa \Garcia Ramirez\

Entering Locations

Recording locations accurately and completely is an important part of your family history. Generally, you'll enter a location from the smallest to largest division. For example, in the United States, you would enter city or town, county, state, country (Haddam, Washington, Kansas, United States). For foreign locations, you would enter city or town, parish or district, province or county, country (Witton, Aston, Warwickshire, England).

- To help you enter locations quickly and consistently, Family Tree Maker has a locations database that includes more than 3 million place names. When you type a location, Family Tree Maker checks the name against the database and suggests possible matches. You can select a location from the list or add your own place names.

- Click the **Go to Place** icon next to a place field to open the Places workspace and center the map on the corresponding location.

Adding a Spouse

1.   Click **Add Spouse** in the family group view. In the field that appears, enter the spouse's name (first, middle, and last) and click **OK**. Don't forget to use maiden names for women.

Entering Dates

Family Tree Maker automatically converts dates to the standard format used by genealogists: date, month, year. For example, 26 May 1961. If the program can't interpret the date you entered, a message asks for clarification. Simply retype the date in the standard format.

If you don't know the date for an event, you can leave the Date field blank or type "Unknown". If you have an approximate date, you can indicate this by typing "About 1920" or "Abt. 1920".

2. Choose a gender from the drop-down list and click **OK**. The spouse is now the focus of the tree viewer and editing panel.

3. Enter any basic facts (such as birth and death) you have for the new spouse.

Entering Details About a Relationship

After you've entered a spouse for an individual, you'll want to include any additional information you have about the couple. You can enter shared facts (such as marriage or divorce), notes, and media items (such as wedding photos).

1. Go to the **Tree** tab on the People workspace and select the appropriate individual.

2. To add a marriage date and place, simply enter the information in the appropriate fields.

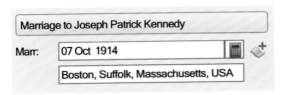

3. To enter more information for the couple, click the **Marriage to** button; then click a tab to enter facts, notes, or media items.

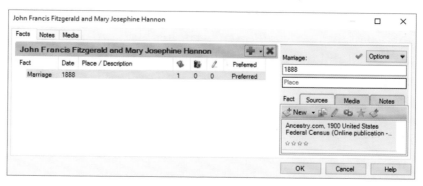

Adding a Child to a Family

1. In the family group view, click **Add Child**. Then, enter the child's name (first, middle, and last) and click **OK**.

    Tip: Family Tree Maker assumes that a child has the same last name as the father and automatically fills it in for you. You can ignore the suggested name by typing over it.

2. In the editing panel, choose a gender and enter any birth and death information you have for the child.

Changing the Sort Order of Children

You can change the order in which children appear in the family group view. For example, your direct ancestor can be displayed at the top of the list regardless of his or her birth order, or you can display all children by birth order. You can change the sort order of children only when the **Show blended families** option is turned off (see page 54 for more information).

1. Go to the **Tree** tab on the People workspace and select the appropriate family.

2. Click a child in the family group view.

3. Do one of the following:

   - Click the **Move child up** ▲ and **Move child down** ▼ buttons to move a child to a specific place in the order.

   - Click the **Sort children by birth order** ⟳ button to display the children in their birth order. Choose whether you want to sort this family only or all children in your tree. Then click **OK**.

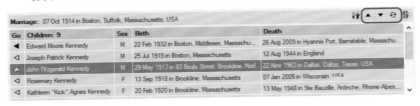

Adding Parents

When you've added your spouse and children to your tree, you'll want to continue with your parents, grandparents, great-grandparents, and so on.

1. Go to the **Tree** tab on the People workspace. In the Index or tree viewer, click the individual you want to add a father or mother to.

2.   Click **Add Father** or **Add Mother** in the tree viewer.

3.   Enter the parent's name (first, middle, and last). Don't forget to use maiden names for women.

4.   In the editing panel, choose a gender and enter any birth and death information you have for the individual.

Adding More Details

So far, you've only entered basic facts for a person. Now you can add more details and notes.

Adding a Fact

In addition to birth and death events, you can add facts such as christenings, immigration, and occupations.

Note: You'll want to record the source of each fact. A source is where you learned the information such as a book or historical record. For more information, see Chapter 5 (page 71).

1.   Go to the **Tree** tab on the People workspace and select the appropriate individual. Then click the **Person** tab.

2. Click the **Facts** button. The facts you've already entered for the person appear in the **Individual & Shared Facts** section.

3. Right-click the workspace and select **Add Fact**, or click the **Add fact (+)** button in the toolbar. The Add Fact window opens.

4. Choose a fact from the list and click **OK**.

Tip: You can add your own fact types (for example, college graduation) by clicking the **New** button in the Add Fact window.

Notice that the editing panel on the right-hand side of the window displays the appropriate fields for the fact.

5. Complete the **Date**, **Place**, and **Description** fields as necessary.

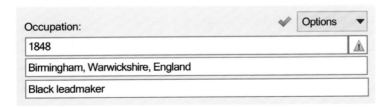

Note: Don't forget to add a source for the fact. For instructions see "Creating Sources" on page 73.

Common Facts

In addition to birth, marriage, and death events, here are some facts you will probably encounter as you record your family history:

- **Address.** Addresses can be useful for keeping contact information for living relatives or for recording where an ancestor lived.

- **Also Known As.** Use this fact if an individual was known by a nickname rather than his or her given name.

- **Baptism and Christening.** Birth records are not always available, so christening records become useful because they may be the earliest available information you can find for an ancestor.

- **Burial.** If you can't find a death record for an individual, but you have a burial record, you can use this information to estimate a person's death date.

- **Cause of Death/Medical Condition.** Knowing your family's health history may help you prevent and treat illnesses that run in families. You can record an individual's cause of death or enter details you know about an individual's medical history, from long-term illness to simple things such as "suffers from allergies."

- **Emigration/Immigration.** Emigration and immigration records are the first step in finding your ancestors in their homeland. Use these facts to record dates, ports of departure and arrival, and even ship names.

- **Physical Description.** Although not necessarily beneficial to your research, a physical description of an ancestor can be a fascinating addition to any family history.

- **Title.** If an individual has a title, such as Captain, you can use it to tell the difference between this individual and others with the same or similar names.

Copying and Pasting Facts

You can copy a fact from one person and paste it into the facts for another person. This is useful if several family members share the same fact (such as residence), and you don't want to create a new fact for each person.

1. Go to the **Tree** tab on the People workspace and select the appropriate individual. Then click the **Person** tab.

2. Click the **Facts** button.

3. Right-click the fact you want to copy and select **Copy**.

4. Use the mini pedigree tree above the workspace to go to the person you want to add the fact to.

5. Right-click the **Individual & Shared Facts** section and select **Paste**. A list of immediate family members appears.

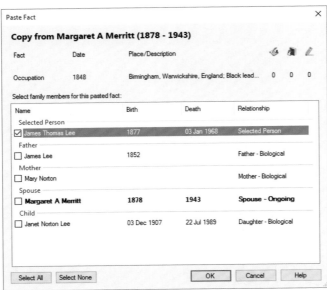

6. Click the checkboxes next to each person you want to add the fact to; then click **OK**.

Adding Alternate Facts

As you add facts, you may discover conflicting information about the same life event, such as two birth dates. When you have multiple facts for the same event, one fact will be "preferred," and the others will be "alternates." In figure 4-1 the birth has one preferred fact and two alternate facts.

Fact	Date	Place / Description				Preferred
Personal Information						
Name		JFK	0	0	0	
Name		Jack	1	0	0	
Name		John Fitzgerald Kennedy	6	1	0	Preferred
Sex		Male	0	0	0	Preferred
Individual Facts						
Birth	1917	New Hackensack, Dutchess, New York, USA	0	0	0	
Birth	29 May 1917	Brookline, Norfolk, Massachusetts, USA; Kennedy was born at 83 Beals Street in Brookli...	5	1	0	Preferred
Birth	29 May 1918	Albuquerque, New Mexico, USA; no source information can be found for this, but some say it...	0	0	0	
Burial	25 Nov 1963	Arlington National Cemetery	0	0	0	Preferred
Cause of Death		tragic.	0	0	0	Preferred
Death	22 Nov 1963	Minnesota	1	0	0	
Death	22 Nov 1963	Dallas, Dallas, Texas, USA	2	0	0	Preferred
Military Service		He served in WWII	0	0	0	Preferred
Occupation	Abt. 1960	Washington, DC; President	0	0	0	Preferred
Religion	Aft. 1933	Catholic	1	0	0	Preferred
Residence	Bef. 1920	Brookline, Norfolk, Massachusetts	2	0	0	
Residence	Bet. 1930–1931	Bronxville, Westchester, New York	1	1	0	Preferred

Figure 4-1. Alternate facts on the Person tab.

Note: An alternate fact doesn't have to include conflicting information. For example, you may have three Address facts for an individual, all of which are correct.

Choosing a Preferred Fact

When you enter multiple facts for the same life event, you'll have to choose which fact is preferred. Typically, this is the fact that is the most accurate or complete. Preferred facts are shown by default in the editing panel, charts, and reports.

1. Go to the **Tree** tab on the People workspace and select the appropriate individual. Then click the **Person** tab.

2. Click the **Facts** button; then click the fact you want to make preferred.

3. In the editing panel, click the **Options** button and choose **Preferred** from the drop-down list.

The Preferred column in the **Individual & Shared Facts** section now shows the fact as preferred.

Tip: You can also set a preferred fact by right-clicking the fact and choosing **Set As Preferred** from the drop-down list.

Making a Fact Private

You may enter facts that you don't want to share with other family members or researchers. If you make a fact private, you can choose whether or not to include it in reports and when you export a tree.

1. Go to the **Tree** tab on the People workspace and select the appropriate individual. Then click the **Person** tab.

2. Click the **Facts** button; then click the fact you want to be private.

3.   In the editing panel, click the **Options** button and choose
Mark as Private from the drop-down list.

A lock 🔒 icon will appear next to the private fact in the **Individual & Shared Facts** section (fig. 4-2).

Individual Facts

Birth	28 Jul 1929	Southampton, New York
Arrival	30 Aug 1948	New York, New York
🔒 Religion	Abt. 1968	New York, New York; 1865
Death	19 May 1994	New York
Departure		Cherbourg, France

Figure 4-2. A lock icon indicates that a fact is private.

Adding a Note for an Individual

You may have family stories, legends, or research resources that you
want to refer to occasionally. Family Tree Maker lets you enter this
type of information in notes—up to 1MB of space, or about 200
printed pages, per note.

Tip: If you are entering notes from another document on your computer,
you can "copy and paste" so you don't have to retype existing text.

Entering a Personal Note

Personal notes may be as simple as a physical description or as lengthy as a transcript of an interview with your grandmother.

Note: You should *not* record source information on the Notes tab; if you do, the information won't be included in source reports.

1. Go to the **Tree** tab on the People workspace and select the appropriate individual. Then click the **Person** tab.

2. Click the **Notes** tab at the bottom of the Person tab. Then click the **Person note** button in the Notes toolbar.

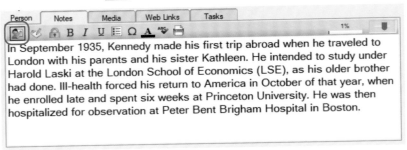

3. Place the cursor in the notes area and enter your text. You can press **Enter** to start a new paragraph.

Entering a Research Note

Sometimes a record or family story will give you clues that can help you learn more about your family. You can create research notes to remind you of the next steps you want to take.

1. Go to the **Tree** tab on the People workspace and select the appropriate individual. Then click the **Person** tab.

2. Click the **Notes** tab at the bottom of the Person tab; then click the **Research note** 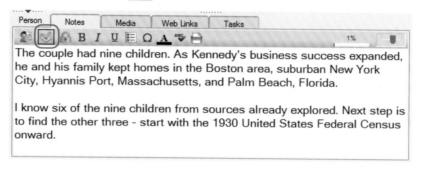 button in the Notes toolbar.

3. Place the cursor in the notes area and enter your text.

Changing a Note's Display Size

You can resize your notes to make the text larger and easier to read or make the text smaller to fit more words on the tab. Simply drag the slider on the right side of the Notes toolbar (fig. 4-3). This only changes how the note is displayed it does not affect how it prints.

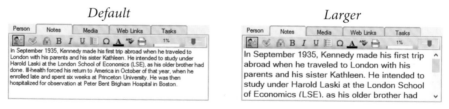

Figure 4-3. A slider on the Notes tab lets you resize the text.

Printing a Note

To print a note, click the printer button on the Notes toolbar. Select your printing options and click **OK**.

Tip: You can also create a report of any notes you've entered in your tree. Go to the Publish workspace and choose **Person Reports**. Then double-click **Notes Report**.

Making a Note Private

You may have information about a relative that you don't want to share with other researchers. If you make a note private, you can choose whether or not to include it in reports and when you export a tree.

After entering a note, click the **Mark as Private** button. You can tell the note has been marked as private because the lock icon will have a black box around it with an orange background.

Figure 4-4. The Mark as Private button in its two states.

Adding Web Links for an Individual

If you want to keep track of a website you found about an ancestor or an interesting collection of online maps, you can create a Web link so you can easily access it again.

1.   Go to the **Tree** tab on the People workspace and select the appropriate individual. Then click the **Person** tab.

2.   Click the **Web Links** tab at the bottom of the Person tab; then click the **New** button in the toolbar.

3.   Enter the address for the website.

    Note: Family Tree Maker Web links cannot be synced with Web links in your Ancestry tree at this time. See "Differences between FTM and Ancestry trees" on page 236.

4.   Enter a name for the link and click **OK**.

Color Coding

When you are working on a large tree, it can sometimes be difficult to trace family lines through the generations without creating a relationship report. To help you see lineages at a glance, Family Tree Maker allows you to use color coding to mark all the direct-line ancestors and descendants of any given person. The coloring scheme is based on the classic four-color system created by Mary E. V. Hill, but has been further extended to give you more coloring options.

You can highlight a selected person's descendants with one color and his or her ancestors with another. Or, for ancestors, you can use a four-color system to apply different colors to four different lineages: the paternal father's line, the paternal mother's line, the maternal father's line, and the maternal mother's line.

You can apply one of the four-color choices to one parent, and another four-color palette to another parent, producing the full eight colors in the tree viewer.

Figure 4-5. Pedigree view with applied color coding.

Applying color coding to a person in your tree

1.   Go to the **Tree** tab on the **People** workspace.

2.   Select the person you want to highlight or whose ancestors and descendants you want to highlight.

3.   Click the **Color Coding** button above the editing panel.

4.   Click a color or a color group for the type of individuals to whom you want to apply color coding: **Current Person, All Ancestors (1 color), All Ancestors (4 colors),** or **All Descendants.**

   Colored bars now appear on all the relevant person thumbnails in the tree viewer. Colored dots are also shown next to the corresponding names in the Index and in the lists of people on the Places, Media, and Sources workspaces.

   If you have applied color coding for several selected individuals in your tree, there may be some people who belong to more than one family line—in this case all the corresponding colors will be displayed on those individuals' thumbnails. To find out why a person is marked with a particular color, hold the pointer over the colored bar on his or her thumbnail. A help tag will appear with the explanation.

Another great way to use color coding is as an attribute of a certain criterion—in other words, an additional, at-a-glance filter. For example, you can create a filter of all persons who served in the military, or lived in a certain location, then assign a color to that attribute and save your filter. That allows you to easily see the individuals that satisfy that criterion both in the Index panel and in the tree viewer. To learn more about creating filters, see "The Index" on page 12.

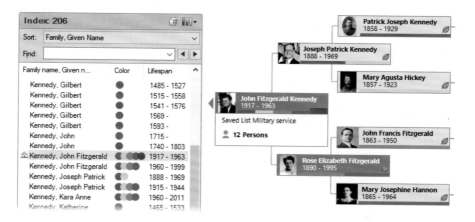

Removing color coding for an individual or individual's lineage

1. On the **Tree** tab of the **People** workspace, select a person to whom color coding has been applied.

2. Click the **Color Coding** button above the editing panel.

3. Click the **No Color** ☒ button for the color coding that you want to remove.

To remove all color coding from your tree, click the **Color Coding** button above the editing panel, and then click **Clear All Colors**.

Working with Relationships

As you dig deeper into your family history you will discover individuals who marry multiple times, divorces, adoptions, and other special situations. Family Tree Maker can handle all different types of relationships.

Using the Combined Family View

The family group view on the People workspace displays a couple and their mutual children. You can change this view so it displays all children associated with the couple, including children from previous marriages and relationships.

Note: When you display a "blended family" in the family group view, you cannot change the sort order of the children; they will be listed chronologically by birth date.

1. Go to the **Tree** tab on the People workspace and select the appropriate family.

2. Click the **Show blended families** button in the family group view.

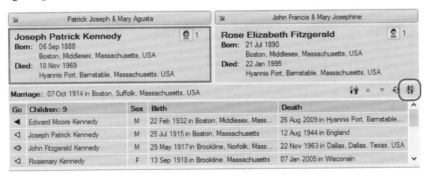

The combined family group view now displays all the children of both individuals. An icon to the left of the child's name indicates whether he or she is the child of the father, the mother, or both parents.

3. To return to the traditional family group view, simply click the **Show blended families** button again.

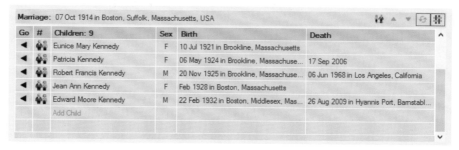

Viewing an Individual's Family Relationships

You can see all the members of an individual's family at a glance—spouses, children, parents, and siblings.

1. Go to the **Person** tab on the People workspace and select the appropriate individual.

2. Click the **Relationships** button. You can now see parents, siblings, spouses, and children entered for the individual.

Adding Additional Spouses

If an individual in your family has been married more than once, you'll want to enter all additional spouses.

1. Go to the **Tree** tab on the People workspace.

2. Select the appropriate individual.

3. In the family group view, click the **Choose spouse** icon next to the individual. From the drop-down list, you can view the existing spouse or create a new spouse.

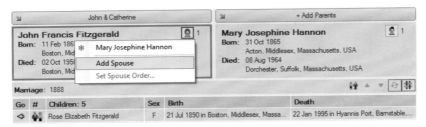

4. Choose **Add Spouse** from the drop-down list.

5. Enter the name of the new spouse and click **OK**.

6. Family Tree Maker displays a new family group view—this time with the new spouse.

7. To view the first spouse again, click the **Choose spouse** icon and choose his or her name from the drop-down list.

Choosing a Preferred Spouse

If you enter more than one spouse for an individual, you need to indicate who is the preferred spouse. (Usually this is the spouse whose children are in your direct family line.) The preferred spouse will become the default spouse displayed in the family group view, tree viewer, and charts and reports.

1. Go to the **Tree** tab on the People workspace and select the appropriate individual.

2. Click the **Person** tab; then click the **Relationships** button. You should see two or more names under the Spouses heading.

3. Click the individual you want to be the preferred spouse. Then, in the editing panel, click the **Preferred spouse** checkbox.

Switching Between Spouses

Family Tree Maker displays a person's preferred spouse by default, but you can switch to other spouses when necessary.

1. Go to the **Tree** tab on the People workspace and select the appropriate individual.

2. In the family group view, click the **Choose spouse** 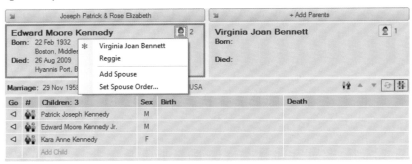 icon next to the individual. From the drop-down list, choose the spouse you want to view.

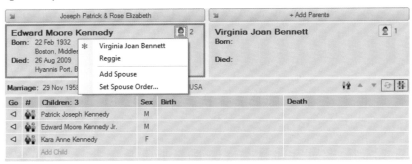

Choosing a Type of Relationship for a Couple

You can choose what type of relationship a couple has (e.g., partner, friend, spouse).

1. Go to the **Tree** tab on the People workspace and select the appropriate couple.

2. Click the **Person** tab; then click the **Relationships** button.

3. Click the spouse's name. Then, in the editing panel, choose a relationship type from the **Relationship** drop-down list.

Choosing a Status for a Couple's Relationship

The status of a couple's relationship will be "Ongoing" by default. If necessary, you can change this status. For example, if a couple gets a divorce, you can indicate this with their relationship status.

1. Go to the **Tree** tab on the People workspace and select the appropriate couple.

2. Click the **Person** tab; then click the **Relationships** button.

3. Click the spouse's name. Then, in the editing panel, choose a status from the **Status** drop-down list.

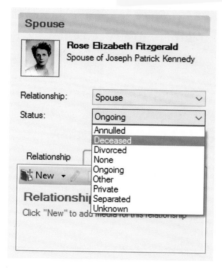

Choosing a Relationship Between Parents and a Child

You can indicate a child's relationship to each of his or her parents (e.g., biological, adopted, foster).

1. Go to the **Tree** tab on the People workspace and select the appropriate individual.

2. Click the **Person** tab; then click the **Relationships** button.

3. Click the father's or mother's name. Then, in the editing panel, choose a relationship from the **Relationship** drop-down list.

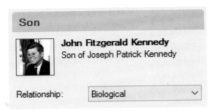

Adding an Unrelated Individual

As you search for family members, you might find a person you suspect is related to you, but you have no proof. You can add this person to your tree without linking them to a specific family. Later on, if you find out that they are related, you can easily link them to the correct family.

1. Click the **People** button on the main toolbar.

2. Click **Person>Add Person>Add Unrelated Person**.

3. Enter the person's name (first, middle, and last). Then choose a gender from the drop-down list and click **OK**.

Viewing a Timeline

Timelines can be a great tool to put the life of your ancestor in context—historical and otherwise. Family Tree Maker has three timeline variations: events in an individual's life; events in the lives of their immediate family (such as birth, marriage, and death); and historical events.

1. Go to the **Person** tab on the People workspace and select the appropriate person. Then click the **Timeline** button.

A chronological list of events is displayed—along with the person's age at the time of each event.

2. To display events for immediate family members, click the down arrow next to the **Timeline** button and select **Show Family Events**.

    Events for the individual are indicated by green markers, and events in his or her family are indicated by pink markers.

3. To display historical events, click the down arrow next to the **Timeline** button and select **Show Historical Events**.

    Historical events are indicated by yellow markers.

4. To learn more about a historical event, click the event. A description appears on the right side of the window.

    Note: Family Tree Maker comes with default historical events that you can edit, delete, and add to. To learn more see "Managing Historical Events" on page 272.

Creating Smart Stories™

Smart Stories is a tool that helps you quickly create stories about individuals and families using the facts, notes, and photos in your tree. And because Smart Stories are linked to the tree, you can edit a fact and the text in your story will be updated automatically. For example, if you find out that grandfather's birth date is different than you thought, change it in your tree and the story will be updated at the same time.

Family Tree Maker can automatically generate a Smart Story for an individual (fig. 4-4). It will have an image of the person (if you've added a portrait), the individual's immediate family (children,

Joseph Patrick Kennedy

Joseph Patrick Kennedy was born on 06 Sep 1888 in Boston, Middlesex, Massachusetts, USA as the fourth child of Patrick Joseph Kennedy and Mary Agusta Hickey. He had three siblings, namely: Francis, Loretta, and Margaret. He died on 18 Nov 1969 in Hyannis Port, Barnstable, Massachusetts, USA. When he was 26, he married Rose Elizabeth Fitzgerald, daughter of John Francis Fitzgerald and Mary Josephine Hannon, on 07 Oct 1914 in Boston, Suffolk, Massachusetts, USA.

Joseph Patrick Kennedy lived in Brookline, Norfolk, Massachusetts in 1920. He lived in Bronxville, Westchester, New York in 1930. He arrived in New York, New York on 15 Dec 1938. He departed from Southampton, England.

Joseph Patrick Kennedy and Rose Elizabeth Fitzgerald had the following children:

1. Edward Moore Kennedy was born on 22 Feb 1932 in Boston, Middlesex, Massachusetts, USA. He died on 26 Aug 2009 in Hyannis Port, Barnstable, Massachusetts, USA. He married Virginia Joan Bennett on 29 Nov 1958 in Bronxville, Westchester, New York, USA.
2. Joseph Patrick Kennedy was born on 25 Jul 1915 in Boston, Massachusetts. He died on 12 Aug 1944 in England.
3. John Fitzgerald Kennedy was born on 29 May 1917 in Brookline, Norfolk, Massachusetts, USA (Kennedy was born at 83 Beals Street in Brookline, Massachusetts on Tuesday, May 29, 1917, at 3:00 p.m.). He died on 22 Nov 1963 in Dallas, Dallas, Texas, USA. He married Jacqueline Lee Bouvier on 12 Sep 1953 in Newport, Newport, Rhode Island, USA (The couple were married on September 12, 1953 at St. Mary's Church in Newport, Rhode Island. The 11 a.m. ceremony was officiated by Archbishop Richard Cushing. A whopping 750 guests attended, with an additional 3,000 well-wishers who waited outside).
4. Rosemary Kennedy was born on 13 Sep 1918 in Brookline, Massachusetts. She died on 07 Jan 2005 in Wisconsin.
5. Kathleen "Kick" Agnes Kennedy was born on 20 Feb 1920 in Brookline, Massachusetts. She died on 13 May 1948 in Ste Bauzille, Ardeche, Rhone-Alpes, France.
6. Eunice Mary Kennedy was born on 10 Jul 1921 in Brookline, Massachusetts. She married Robert Sargent Shriver on 23 May 1953.
7. Patricia Kennedy was born on 06 May 1924 in Brookline, Massachusetts. She died on 17 Sep 2006. She married Peter Sydney Lawford on 24 Apr 1954.

Figure 4-6. A Smart Story created by Family Tree Maker.

spouses, parents, and siblings), and their life events. You can also create your own Smart Stories, starting with a blank page and adding your own images and text.

You can create Smart Stories on an individual's Media tab, the Media workspace, or the Publish workspace. All stories can be printed, exported, and included in family history books; however, if you upload your tree to Ancestry, Smart Stories created on the Publish workspace are considered reports and won't be uploaded.

Creating a Smart Story as a Media Item

1. Select the individual you want to create a Smart Story for.

2. Do one of the following:

    • Go to the **Person** tab for an individual and click the **Media** tab at the bottom of the window. Click the **New** button and choose **Create New Smart Story** from the drop-down menu.

    • Go to the Media workspace. Then select **Media>Create a New Smart Story**.

3. If you want Family Tree Maker to generate the story for you, click **Auto-populate Smart Story**. To create your own story, click **Start with blank page**.

4. Click **OK**.

Creating a Smart Story as a Report

1. Go to the **Collection** tab on the Publish workspace. In Publication Types, click **Other**.

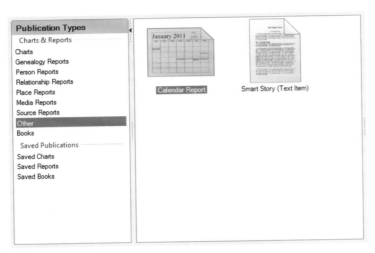

2. Double-click the **Smart Story** icon. The editor opens.

Tip: To access this Smart Story later, go to the Publish workspace and select **Saved Reports**.

Including a Short Biography

1. Place the cursor where you want to add a biography.
2. Click the **Facts** [icon] button on the Smart Stories toolbar. Then choose "Personal Biography" from the drop-down list.

3. By default a title, photo, and the individual's immediate family (children, spouses, parents, and siblings) will be included. Deselect the checkboxes for items you don't want.

4. Click the **Insert** button.

Including Facts

1. Place the cursor on the page where you want to add a fact.

2. Click the **Facts** button on the Smart Stories toolbar. Then choose "Facts" from the drop-down list.

3. Select the fact you want to add to your story. Below the fact, you'll see options of how the fact will be entered. You can create a sentence or add specific details.

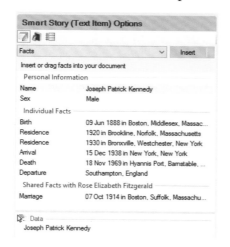

4. Drag the text to your document or click the **Insert** button.

    Tip: To include the facts, media items, or notes from another person in your tree, click the file folder icon in the top corner and choose a different person.

Including Sources

1. Place the cursor on the page where you want to add a source.

2. Click the **Facts** button on the Smart Stories toolbar. Then choose "Fact Sources" from the drop-down list.

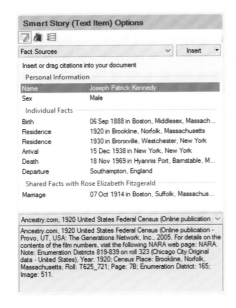

3. Click the fact that has the source you want to add to your story. Below you'll see any associated source citations. If more than one source citation exists for a fact, you can choose it from a drop-down list.

4. Drag the text to your document or click the **Insert** button.

Including Notes

1. Place the cursor on the page where you want to add a note.
2. Click the **Facts** button on the Smart Stories toolbar. Then choose "Notes" from the drop-down list.

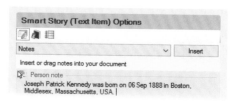

3. Drag the text to your document or click the **Insert** button.

Including Images

1. Place the cursor on the page where you want to add a media item.
2. Click the **Media** button on the Smart Stories toolbar.

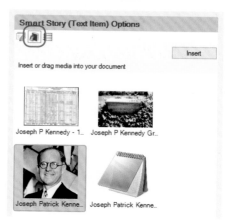

3. Select the media item you want to use.
4. Drag the image to your document or click the **Insert** button.

Creating Timelines

You can use facts in a person's life and historical events to create a timeline.

1. Place the cursor on the page where you want to add an event.

2. Click the **Timeline** button on the Smart Stories toolbar. Then choose an event type from the drop-down list.

3. Click the event you want to add to your story. Below the event, you'll see options of how the event will be entered. You can create a sentence or add specific details.

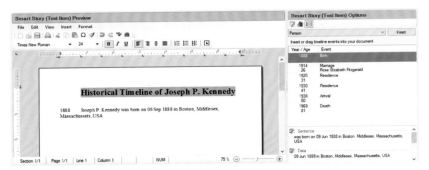

4. Drag the text to your document or click the **Insert** button.

Editing Smart Stories Text

Smart Stories pulls text directly from your tree. That means you don't have to worry about continually redoing your story; if information in your tree changes, your story will be updated automatically.

You can also edit text in Smart Stories. But, be aware that the text will no longer be linked to your tree and will not be updated automatically.

1. Move the cursor over the text you want to add, edit, or delete. You can identify which text is linked to your tree because it will be highlighted.

1888   Joseph P. Kennedy was born on 06 Sep 1888 in Boston, Middlesex, Massachussets, US, were married on 07 Oct 1914 in Boston, Suffolk, Massachussets, USA
He lived in Brookline, Norfolk, Massachussets in 1920

2. Double-click the text block. A message asks whether you want to edit the text.

3. Click **Yes**.

Chapter Five
Documenting Your Research

Documenting sources—recording where you discovered a fact—is one of the most important aspects of your research. Sources are valuable for many reasons. When you cite a source, you are proving to others which records you based your facts on; if you eventually share your research with your family or other researchers, your family history may be judged for accuracy based on your sources. If your sources are detailed and correct, others will be able to follow your research footsteps.

Each time you add information to your tree, you'll want to create a source and source citation that describe where you found the info. For example, if you find your father's birthplace on his World War I draft card, you'll create a source for the record when you add his birth date and birthplace.

Understanding Sources and Source Citations

If you're new to family history, you may not be familiar with sources and source citations. This section gives an explanation of each and also shows you some examples.

- A source is the unchanging facts about an item; for example, the author, title, and publication information for a book.

- Source citations are individual details that explain where you found a fact, such as the page number in a book.

To help you understand how sources and source citations work together, let's look at an example from the 1930 United States Federal Census. First, you would create a source for the census that includes information like this:

- A title—1930 United States Federal Census

- Where you located the source—www.ancestry.com

- Publishing details—Bureau of the Census. Washington, D.C.: National Archives and Records Administration, 1930.

As you can see, these details about the 1930 census won't change regardless of who or what you find in the records. However, because you'll find families and individuals in different locations throughout the census, each census fact will need its own source citation. A source citation for an individual in the 1930 census might include this information:

- Source—1930 United States Federal Census

- Source citation—Harold Reed household, Santa Clara Township, Santa Clara County, California. Roll: 219; Page: 14A; Enumeration district: 110.

A source citation for a different individual in the 1930 census might look like this. (Notice the source is the same as the previous example.)

- Source—1930 United States Federal Census

- Source citation—Michael Reed household, Kokomo Township, Beaver County, Oklahoma. Roll: 1892; Page: 5B; Enumeration district: 26.

Both individuals can be found in the 1930 census (the source), but the source citation for each individual has changed because the individuals were recorded in different places in the source.

Creating Sources

Family Tree Maker lets you create sources in two ways: using templates or a basic format. Source templates are useful because you don't have to guess which details need to be entered. Choose the type of source you're creating (for example an obituary) and Family Tree Maker displays the relevant fields. If you don't want to use a template (for example, because you have your own system of citation or you can't find a matching template), you can create a source by completing the standard fields (author, title, and publisher) in the basic source format.

Adding a Source for a Fact

Usually, you will add a source as you create a source citation for a fact or event. This section focuses on adding a source while entering facts on the Tree tab in the People workspace.

Note: You need to create only one source for each item; you can use a source for as many source citations as necessary.

1. Go to the **Tree** tab on the People workspace.

2. In the editing panel, position the pointer over the fact you want to add a source to, click the **New source citation** button that appears next to it, and then choose **Add New Source Citation** from the drop-down list.

3. The Add Source Citation window opens. To create a source using a template, follow the instructions in "Creating a Source from a Template" below. To create a basic source, refer to the "Creating a Source Using the Basic Format" section on page 77.

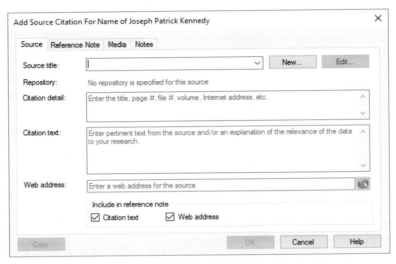

Using Source Templates

Family Tree Maker has more than 170 templates to help you source everything from embroidered samplers and other artifacts to online databases and vital records. These source templates are based on the QuickCheck models used in Elizabeth Shown Mills's book *Evidence Explained*—the premier reference for citing genealogy sources.

Creating a Source from a Template

Using a source template is simple. To determine which template you should use, enter keywords and choose from a list of suggestions, or view a list of all available templates and choose the one that fits best.

To choose a template using keywords

1. Access the Add Source Citation window and click **New**. (For help see "Adding a Source for a Fact" on page 73.)

2. Enter a keyword in the **Source template** field and choose a template from the list of options that appear. To narrow the list, enter multiple keywords. For example, "property" brings up eleven results, while "property grant" brings up one result.

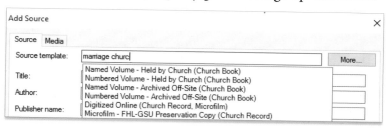

3. The fields that appear now reflect the template you've chosen. Complete these fields as necessary and click **OK**.

You can now add a source citation for the fact (see page 79).

To choose a template from a list

1. Access the Add Source Citation window and click **New**. (If you need help see "Adding a Source for a Fact" on page 73). The Add Source window opens.

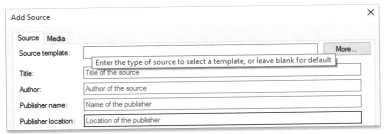

2. Click **More**.

3. In **Source group**, choose the group that most closely matches the item you're sourcing. The categories list changes to reflect the selected source group.

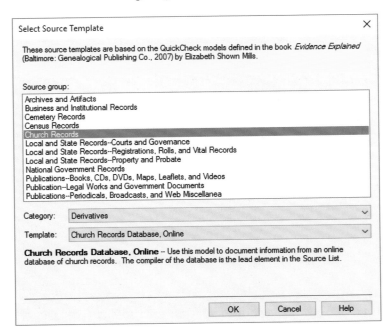

4. Choose the appropriate category from the **Category** drop-down list. The templates list changes to reflect the selected source group and category.

5. Choose a template from the **Template** drop-down list. A description of the template is displayed beneath its title.

6. Click **OK** to return to the Add Source window; the fields that appear now reflect the template you've chosen. Complete these fields as necessary and click **OK**. You can now add a source citation for the fact (see page 79).

Creating a Source Using the Basic Format

If you don't want to use a source template, you can create a source by completing some standard fields (such as author, title, and publisher) in the basic source format.

1. Access the Add Source Citation window and click **New**. (If you need help see "Adding a Source for a Fact" on page 73.) The Add Source window opens.

2.   Complete the source fields as necessary:

  •   **Title.** Enter the title of the source exactly as it appears in the source.

  •   **Author.** Enter the author or originator's name.

  •   **Publisher name.** Enter the name of the publishing company.

  •   **Publisher location.** Enter the place of publication (for example, London, England).

  •   **Publish date.** Enter the copyright date for the source (usually only a year).

  •   **Source repository.** Create a new repository or choose one from the drop-down list.

      A repository is the location where an original source exists. This could be a library, county courthouse, or cousin's home. To create a repository, click **New**. Then enter the name, address, email, and phone number for the location.

  •   **Call number.** Enter a call number, if one exists.

      The call number is the number assigned to the source at the repository. It could be a microfilm number, a Dewey Decimal system number, or some other numbering system unique to a particular library or archive.

  •   **Comments.** Enter any comments about the source and the information found in it. This information will not print on your reports; it is for your personal reference. You might include a description of the item or information about its legibility.

3.   Click **OK**. You can now add a source citation for the fact (see page 79).

Creating Source Citations

After you create a source, you're ready to identify where in the source you found information by creating a source citation. Family Tree Maker lets you create source citations in a variety of ways; you'll need to decide which method is most effective for you.

Note: You can have more than one source citation for the same fact. For example, you might find an immigration date for your great-grandmother on a naturalization record and a census record. You should make source citations for both records.

Adding a New Source Citation

Each time you add a fact to your tree, you should take a minute to document where you discovered the information, whether it's a book in a library or a record you found online. When you create a new source citation, you'll link it to a source and add any additional identifying information such as page or volume number.

1. Access the Add Source Citation window. (If you need help see "Adding a Source for a Fact" on page 73.)

2.   Change the citation as necessary:

   •   **Source title.** From the drop-down list, choose the source of the information.

   •   **Citation detail.** Enter details about where you found the information in the source, such as a page number.

   •   **Citation text.** Enter any additional information. For example, you might enter a quote from a book or add a paraphrased summary of the source text.

   •   **Web address.** For online sources, enter the URL where the information was found.

   •   **Include in reference note.** Select the **Citation text** checkbox to include text in the Citation text field in printed reference notes. Select the **Web address** checkbox to include the source's URL in printed reference notes. (The source title and citation detail are always included in reference notes.)

   You can include a media item or note as part of a source citation. For instructions, see "Attaching a Media Item to a Source Citation" on page 84 and "Adding a Note to a Source Citation" on page 85.

3.   Click **OK**.

Linking a Fact to an Existing Source Citation

If you've already created a citation for a source, such as a death certificate, you don't have to create another source citation for each fact or individual in the source. For example, if you find your grandparents' names and birthplaces in your aunt's death certificate, you don't have to create a new source citation for the death certificate; you can simply link these facts to the citation you already created.

1.   Go to the **Person** tab on the People workspace and select the appropriate individual.

2. Click the fact to which you want to add a source citation to
    select it.

3. On the **Sources** tab of the editing panel, click the down arrow
    next to the **New** button and choose **Use Existing Source Cita-
    tion** from the drop-down list.

The Find Source Citation window opens.

4. Click the citation you want to link to from the list.

5. Click **Link to Citation**. The citation information now appears on the Sources tab.

Copying and Updating a Source Citation

If you need to create a source citation that is similar to one already in your tree, don't make a new citation. Simply copy the old one and update details as necessary (such as a page number). For example, if several family members are in the same city directory for Cleveland, Ohio, you can create a source citation for one family, then copy and update the source citation for other families in the directory.

1. Go to the **Person** tab on the People workspace and select the appropriate individual.

2. Click the fact to which you want to add a source citation to select it.

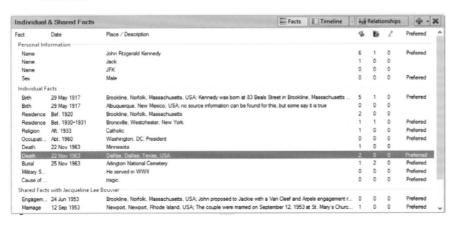

3. On the **Sources** tab of the editing panel, click the down arrow next to the **New** button and choose **Use Existing Source Citation** from the drop-down list. The Find Source Citation window opens.

4. Click the citation you want to copy from the list.

5. Click **Create New Copy**. A citation link appears on the Sources tab. Now you can edit the citation without affecting the original.

6. Double-click the source citation to open it in an editing window. Then make any necessary changes and click **OK**.

Attaching a Media Item to a Source Citation

If you have an image or recording of a source, you can link it to a source citation. For example, you might have a scan of a marriage certificate or census record that you want to add to the source citation.

1. Double-click a source citation to open it in an editing window.

2. In the dialog that appears, click the **Media** tab.

3. Do one of the following:

    •   If the media item is already in your tree, click **Link To Existing Media**. Click the item you want then click **OK**.

    •   To add a media item, click **Attach New Media**. Use the file management window to navigate to the media item. Then click **Open**.

4. In the **Copy to Media Folder** dialog that appears, choose whether you want to create an additional copy of the file in a your tree's media folder or to link to the file on your computer only, and then click **OK**.

5. Click **OK**.

Adding a Note to a Source Citation

You can use the Notes tab for additional information you have about a source that you weren't able to include elsewhere. For example, you can enter a note about how you discovered a source or where the source is located.

1. Double-click a source citation to open it in an editing window.

2. Click the **Notes** tab in a source citation.

3. Enter a note and click **OK**.

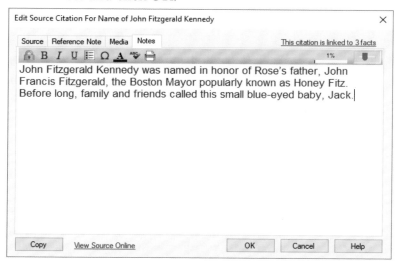

Using Source Repositories

With most sources, it's possible to specify the physical location where the original source can be found. This could be a library, county courthouse, or an individual's home. This location is called the source's repository. Naturally, more than one source may reside in a repository. Therefore, you only need to enter information on each repository once. You can then link the appropriate sources to it rather than retyping the information for each source you create.

Adding a Repository

1. Open the **Add/Edit Source** dialog (see "Adding a Source for a Fact" on page 73.)

2. Click the **New** button next to the **Source repository** drop-down list.

3. In the dialog that appears, enter the name, address, phone number, and email address of the location, and then click **OK**.

Managing Repositories

You can monitor the usage of repositories in your tree, as well as edit repository information, delete repositories, and add new ones. Changes you make to a repository are automatically applied to all the sources that are linked to it.

Reviewing Usage of a Repository

You may need to know how much information in your tree is sourced from a specific repository or to check that a repository has the correct sources linked to it. To do that, follow these steps:

1. Open the **Repositories** dialog by choosing **Manage Repositories** from the **Edit** menu.

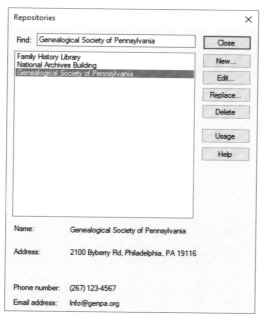

2. Select a repository and click **Usage**. The **Repository Usage** dialog will appear with a list of sources linked to the selected repository and citations for these sources.

Replacing a Repository

You can change all of the occurrences of one repository to another repository. This merges the two repositories together as the second repository and deletes the first repository. All of the sources previously linked to the first repository will now be linked to the second repository. This allows you to combine duplicate repositories into a single repository without reassigning each source.

1. In the **Repositories** dialog, select the repository you want to replace.

2. Click the **Replace** button.

3. In the dialog that appears, select the repository to which you want to link all sources from the first repository.

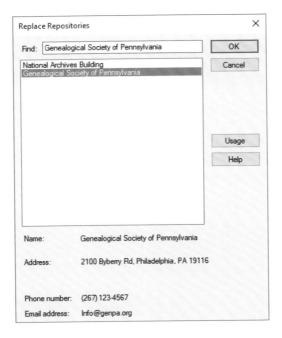

4. Click **OK**. In the alert message that appears, click **Yes.**

Editing Repository Information

To update or correct information about a particular repository, follow these steps:

1. Open the **Repositories** dialog by choosing **Manage Repositories** from the **Edit** menu.

2. Select the repository you want to edit.

3. Click the **Edit** button.

4. Change the name, address, phone number, and/or email address, and then click **OK**.

Deleting a Repository

1. In the **Repositories** dialog, select the repository you want to delete.

2. Click the **Delete** button.

3. In the message that appears, click **Yes** to unlink all sources from the repository and delete it.

Chapter Six
Including Media Items

As you gather names, dates, and facts, you'll realize that they tell only part of your family's story. In order to really bring your ancestors to life, you'll want to illustrate your family history with photographs, important documents, and video and sound clips.

Family Tree Maker helps you organize your multimedia items in one central location. You can link media items to specific individuals; record important notes about each item; use images in family tree charts; and more.

What Media Items Can I Add to My Tree?

Photographs are usually the first thing that comes to mind when you want to illustrate your family history. But don't limit yourself; many personal objects can be scanned or photographed. Here are some items you might want to add to your tree:

- Important records, such as birth and marriage certificates, censuses, passports, diplomas, obituaries, and family Bibles.
- Photographs of heirlooms or items with sentimental value, such as jewelry, medals, artwork, quilts, christening outfits, and furniture.
- Images of ancestral houses and hometowns, businesses, maps, cemeteries, and headstones.
- Family documents, such as letters, funeral books, diaries, Christmas cards, and newspaper and magazine articles.
- Audio clips of oral histories and family stories.

Adding Media Items

If you have a baby picture of your grandmother or a photo of your grandfather's military uniform, you'll want to add it to your tree. You can add photos, audio files, and videos from your computer or you can scan documents directly into Family Tree Maker.

Adding a Media Item for an Individual

1. Go to the **Person** tab on the People workspace and select the appropriate individual.

2. Click the **Media** tab at the bottom of the window.

3. Click the down arrow next to the **New** button and choose **Add New Media** from the drop-down list.

Note: When you add a media item to Family Tree Maker, the original file is not moved from its location on your computer.

4. Use the file management window to navigate to the media item you want to add to your tree. Then click **Open**.

    Tip: You can select multiple media items by clicking on each file while pressing the CTRL key.

    A message asks whether you want to link the file(s) to your tree or create a copy of the file(s).

5. Click **Copy this file** to create an additional copy of the file in a Family Tree Maker media folder, or click **Link to this file** to link to the file on your computer only.

   Tip: Make copies of your media items if you want all your heritage photos and other media items saved in one central location on your computer. This makes them easier to find and easier to back up.

6. Click the checkbox for the category you want this item to belong to; you can select multiple categories. (For more information, see "Media Categories" on page 103.)

7. Click **OK**. The item is added to the individual's Media tab.

Scanning an Image into Your Tree

If you have images you'd like to add to your tree that aren't already on your computer, you can scan them directly into your tree.

When you scan an image, you'll choose the resolution in which the item will be saved. The higher the resolution, or DPI (dots per inch), the sharper your image—and the larger the file size that will be created. If you plan on viewing your images online or sharing them via email, scan images at a lower resolution such as 72 to 150 DPI; if you want to print images in charts and reports, use a higher resolution such as 200 to 300 DPI.

1. Make sure your scanner is connected to your computer and turned on.

2. Go to the Media workspace and choose **Media>Scan Media**. Family Tree Maker automatically searches for connected scanners.

3. Change any settings and click **Scan**. The image is added to the Media workspace.

Changing the Display of an Image

When you're viewing a photo, you can change how it's displayed by rotating the image or zooming in and out on it.

Go to the **Collection** tab on the Media workspace. Double-click a photo or click the photo and then click the **Detail** tab.

Use these buttons in the image toolbar to change the display:

Click the **Rotate right** button to move the image clockwise; click the **Rotate left** button to move the image counterclockwise.

Click the **Magnifier** button to turn the pointer into a magnifying glass when viewing an image.

Click the **Size to fit** button to display the entire image in the current window.

Click the **Actual size** button to show the actual size of the image. You can also choose a specific percentage from the **Fit Image** drop-down list.

Entering Details for a Media Item

After you add a media item, it's a good idea to enter details about it such as a caption, date, and description.

1. Go to the **Collection** tab on the Media workspace. Double-click a media item, or click the image and then click the **Detail** tab.

2. Change the image's details as necessary:

    • **Caption.** Enter a brief title for the item.

    • **Date.** Enter a date for the item. (Typically this is the date the item was created.)

    • **Description.** Describe the media item in detail. For photos you can enter the names of individuals or info about the location depicted; for heirlooms you may want to explain what the item is and its significance to your family.

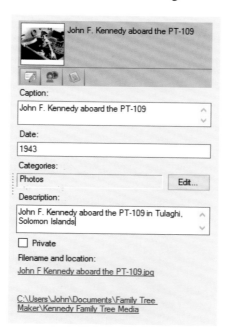

3. Click the **Private** checkbox to keep this media item from being exported or uploaded to your online Ancestry tree.

4. To assign a category to the item, click the **Edit** button next to the **Categories** field. Mark the checkbox for the category you want this item to belong to; you can select multiple categories. Click **OK** when you're finished.

    Tip: You can click the File name and location link to open the Media folder and view the actual media item.

Entering a Note About a Media Item

If you have details that won't fit in a media item's description, you can enter it in the item's notes. For example, a photo of your grand-mother in her graduation robes may include notes about her college education and how you found the image.

1. Go to the **Collection** tab on the Media workspace. Double-click the media item you want to add a note to, or click the image and then click the **Detail** tab.

2. Click the **Notes** tab at the bottom of the window and enter the information.

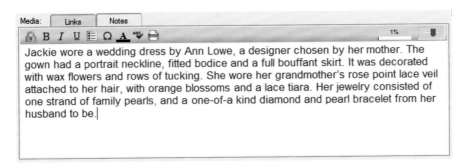

Note: For more information about using notes, see "Adding a Note for an Individual" on page 47.

Adding a Portrait for an Individual

If you want to display a photo of an individual in charts, reports, and the People workspace, you'll need to add a portrait for them.

1. Click the **People** button on the main toolbar. Make sure the individual you want to add a portrait to is the focus of the Tree tab or Person tab.

2. In the editing panel, right-click the person silhouette and do one of the following:

    •   If the photo is already in your tree, click **Link to Existing Picture**. A media item window opens. Click the image you want then click **OK**.

    •   If you're adding a new image, click **Add New Picture**. Use the file management window to navigate to the image you want. Then click **Open**.

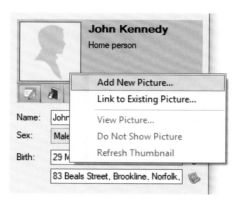

Editing Photos with Photo Darkroom

Old photos may fade and deteriorate with time and wear. Fortunately, Family Tree Maker now comes with a photo repair tool integrated into your genealogy toolkit, to quickly and effortlessly edit your vintage photos without needing to switch to an external image editor. Family Tree Maker's Photo Darkroom is all you need to revive and enhance old photos.

1.   Go to the **Collection** tab on the **Media** workspace. Double-click the photo you want to repair, or select the photo and click the **Detail** tab.

2.   Click the **Photo Darkroom** button. The photo opens in Photo Darkroom.

3.   To view before and after images side by side as you are editing, click the two-pane button in the view control ⬚ ⬚⬚. Both the Result and Original will be displayed.

4. Use the Faded Photo Repair Tool to make the image clearer. Depending on the degree of fading, click the **Light**, **Moderate**, or **Intensive** tool. You can click the tool several times to increase the effect.

5. If you want to make further changes to the photo, open the **Advanced Settings** section by clicking the disclosure triangle, and then drag the **Brightness**, **Contrast**, **Saturation**, and **Sharpness** sliders while observing the changes in the Result view.

6. If you don't like the result of your changes, click the **Undo** button to discard them step by step. You can click the **Restore to Original** button to undo all the changes that you have made to the photo.

7. Click **Done** to apply your changes and return to the **Detail** tab of the **Media** workspace.

Note: The original photo is not modified. It is stored in the **Darkroom Originals** folder in your tree's media folder. If you want to use the original photo in your tree, without the changes that you have made to it, just open the photo in Photo Darkroom at any time, and then click the **Restore to Original** button.

Linking a Media Item to Multiple Individuals

You may have a family photo that includes several individuals in your tree. You don't have to add the picture to each individual; simply add it once to the Media workspace, then link it to the necessary individuals. You can also link media items to specific facts. For example, if you have a photograph of the ship on which your grandparents immigrated to America, you can link the picture to your grandparents and their immigration fact.

1. Go to the **Collection** tab on the Media workspace. Then double-click the item you want to link to multiple individuals, or click the item and then click the **Detail** tab.

2. At the bottom of the Detail tab, you'll see a Links tab. Click the **New** button and choose **Link to Person**.

3. In the **Name** column, click the name of the individual you want to link the item to.

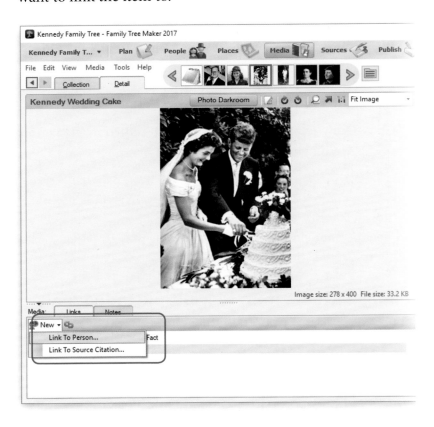

4.   Do one of the following:

- To link the item to a person, click **Link to person only**. (You can link to one person at a time only.)

- To link the item to a specific fact (such as birth), click **Link to person's fact**. Then click the fact in the list below.

5.   Click **OK**.

Tip: If you mistakenly link a media item to an individual, you can unlink it on the Detail tab. Click the appropriate individual and then click the broken link icon in the toolbar.

Managing Media Items

Occasionally you might need to do some maintenance tasks for your media items such as change file names or assign categories.

Opening a Media Item from Family Tree Maker

If you need to edit an image or read a document in your tree, you can open it in its default program without leaving Family Tree Maker.

Go to the **Collection** tab on the Media workspace. Double-click a media item or click the image and click the **Detail** tab. Click the **Open file** button in the image toolbar to open the media item:

 The media item opens in the file's default program. If you edit the media item and save your changes, the modified file will be linked to Family Tree Maker.

Changing a Media Item's File Name

Family Tree Maker lets you change a media item's file name on your computer. This can be useful if you've imported a tree and its media files have generic names; you can use Family Tree Maker to change their file names to something more identifiable.

1. Go to the **Collection** tab on the Media workspace. Right-click a media item and choose **Rename Media File** from the drop-down list, or click a media item and choose **Media>Rename Media File**.

2. Enter the new name for the file and click **OK**.

Arranging an Individual's Media Items

When you add media items for an individual, they are arranged in alphabetical order (by caption). You can change the order in which they appear on the individual's Media tab. For example, you may want to display the pictures by date.

1. Go to the **Person** tab on the People workspace and select the appropriate individual.

2. Click the **Media** tab at the bottom of the window. The tab shows thumbnails of any media items you've linked to this individual.

Use these buttons in the media toolbar to change the display order:

 Click the item you want to move. Then click the **Move Media Forward** and **Move Media Backward** buttons to rearrange the media items. The items will remain in the order you've chosen.

 Click the **Auto Sort Media** button to arrange the media items alphabetically (by caption).

Media Categories

As you add each media item to your tree, you can assign it to categories. These categories make your media items easier to search for, sort, and view.

Creating a Category

You can use the default categories, modify them, or create your own. If you decide to create your own categories, you might want to set up a system before you add your media items. For example, you may want to have event categories (e.g., Weddings, Birthdays, Travel) or categories based on item types (e.g., Photos—Portraits, Movies—Holidays).

1. Go to the **Collection** tab on the Media workspace. In the media editing panel, click the **Edit** button.

2. Click the **Add button**.

3. Enter a name for the category and click **OK**.

Assigning a Category to Multiple Items

Family Tree Maker lets you assign categories to a group of items
at the same time.

1. Go to the **Collection** tab on the Media workspace.

2. Select the media items you want to assign a category to. You
    can select multiple media items by clicking on each file while
    pressing the **CTRL** key.

3. Click **Media>Categorize Media**.

4. In the Categorize Media window, you can choose categories for
    each media item one by one or for all selected media items at once.

Creating a Slide Show

You can create a slide show of pictures you've included in your tree—and even include a soundtrack. You can view your completed slide shows using *Windows Media Player*.

1. Click the **Media** button on the main toolbar. Click **Media>Create Slide Show**.

> Tip: You can create a slide show for a specific individual by clicking the **Create slide show** button on the individual's Media tab.

Kennedy Family Tree_Show   ×

Title (filename):	TLP Family Tree Show
Images to include:	Photos category
	☐ Include relationship media
	☐ Include fact media
Image caption:	Use Captions Only
	18 point Arial, bold, white Font...
Movie size:	Large (800 x 600)
Movie quality:	High
Transition delay:	3.0 ⬍ seconds
Sound track:	C:\Users\John\Music\Run away.mp3 Browse...

Slide show length (based on current settings)

Length of slide show:	3 slides: 0 minutes 9 seconds
Length of sound track:	1 track(s): 0 minutes 0 seconds

Next >   Cancel   Help

2. Change the slide show options as necessary:

- **Title.** Enter a name for the slide show. (This will be the item's file name on your computer also.)

- **Images to include.** To include pictures from a specific category, choose the category name from the drop-down list. Click the **Include relationship media** checkbox to include images linked to relationships; click the **Include fact media** checkbox to include images linked to facts.

- **Image caption.** Choose what text is displayed for images. Click **None** to hide captions; click **Use Captions Only** to display image captions; click **Use Filenames Only** to display file names; click **Use Captions or Filenames** to display captions (if no caption has been entered, the file name will be displayed).

  Click the **Font** button to choose a font style, size, and color for captions and file names used in the slide show.

- **Movie size.** Choose the display size of the slide show from the drop-down list.

  Note: The larger the movie, the more memory required.

- **Movie quality.** Choose the display quality of the slide show from the drop-down list.

  Note: The higher the movie quality, the more memory required.

- **Transition delay.** Choose the number of seconds an image is displayed.

- **Sound track.** To add music to the slide show, click the **Browse** button and locate the MP3 or Windows Media Audio (.wma) file you'd like to use.

3. Click **Next**. Now you can change the order in which images appear or delete images you don't want.

4. Click **Next**. A preview window opens.

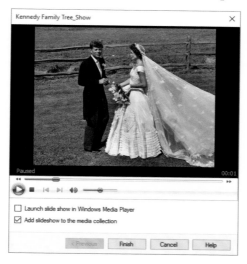

5. Do one of the following:

    •   To view the finished slide show in *Windows Media Player*, click **Launch slide show in Windows Media Player**.

    •   To save the slide show to your tree, click **Add slide show to the media collection**.

6. Click **Finish**.

7. If you have selected the **Add slide show to the media collection** checkbox, the **Copy to Media Folder** dialog appears. Click the checkbox for the category you want this item to belong to; you can select multiple categories. Click **OK** to add the item to the Media workspace.

8. If you have not selected the **Add slide show to the media collection** checkbox, the **Save movie** dialog appears. Choose a location and click **Save**.

Printing a Media Item

1. Go to the **Collection** tab on the Media workspace and click the item you want to print.

2. Click the **Print** button on the main toolbar and choose **Print Media Item** from the drop-down list.

3. When prompted choose a printer, select the number of copies, and choose a page range.

4. Click **Print**.

Chapter Seven
Using Maps

As you gather the names and dates of important events in your ancestors' lives, you'll also record the locations where these events took place—the towns, cities, and countries that shaped their daily lives.

Often, these places exist only as names in a report or on a pedigree chart. Family Tree Maker brings these ancestral homelands to life by letting you virtually visit each place in your tree. For example, you can see satellite images and maps of the town in Denmark where your grandfather was born, the apartment in Chicago where your great-grandparents lived, or even the lake where you went swimming with your cousins every summer.

Each time you enter a location for a fact or event, Family Tree Maker adds it to a "master list" of locations. To view this master list, simply go to the Places workspace. You can then view maps and satellite images of a location, identify individuals in your tree who are associated with certain locations, and more.

Viewing a Map

The interactive online maps in Family Tree Maker are easy to navigate using a few simple tools. You can zoom in and out on the map, change the type of map you're viewing, and more.

Note: You must be connected to the Internet to view these maps.

1.   Click the **Places** button on the main toolbar. To access a map, click a location in the **Places** panel.

There are four map types. The **Road** map type appears by default with the location centered and identified with a red marker. **Aerial** looks straight down at the location. **Bird's eye** provides a 3D angled view. And **Streetside** is the view you'd have standing there. To change the map type, click the map view drop-down menu in the upper right corner and select the view you want.

Microsoft Bing Maps

Family Tree Maker has partnered with Microsoft® *Bing*™ *Maps* to let you access some of the most exciting technology available today. *Bing Maps* takes you beyond typical road maps by combining them with satellite and aerial imagery to let you experience the world as it looks today.

As you visit different locations, you'll notice that the level of detail for each town, region, or country varies. In some areas you can zoom in close enough to see cars, rooftops, and street intersections; in other areas your view will disappear when you get within a mile of the location. Fortunately, *Bing Maps* is updated regularly and regions that may not have many images now will in the future. The most detailed views are of the United States, the United Kingdom, Canada, and Australia.

2.   Choose **Aerial** to view a satellite image of the location.

3. To get a 3D view of a location, click **Bird's eye**. Click the arrows on either side of the compass tool to change the direction of the view.

Note: Bird's eye view is available only for certain parts of the world.

4. To turn the display of map labels such as street names on and off in Aerial and Bird's eye views, click the map view drop-down menu, select **Aerial**, and click the **Labels** switch control at the bottom of the list.

5. Choose **Streetside** to explore places as if you were there. This view is not available for all areas of the world. See "Using Streetside View" on page 114 for more information.

Moving Around a Map

You can quickly change the part of the map you're viewing by dragging it. Move the pointer over the map. When the pointer changes to a hand, click and drag the map in any direction you want.

Zooming In and Out on a Map

You can use the plus and minus buttons on the Map Tools to zoom in and out on the displayed map.

1. Click the plus ⊕ icon to zoom in one level at a time.

2. Click the minus ⊖ icon to zoom out one level at a time.

Using Streetside View

1.   Look for Streetside locations by clicking the map view drop-
     down menu and choosing **Streetside**. The pointer changes to
     the blue man icon wherever Streetside views are available.

2.   Streetside view is not available for all locations. On the map,
     locations that can be viewed from the Streetside perspective
     are shaded blue. If there are any such locations in the display
     area, the Streetside pointer icon is blue. Click the location for
     which you want to get the Streetside view.

3.   If there are no locations with Streetside view in the visible part
     of the map, the Streetside pointer icon turns red. Scroll the
     map until the pointer turns blue or click the Streetside item in
     the map view menu again to toggle off the Streetside pointer
     icon and blue street markings.

4.   In Streetside view, use these means of navigation:

- Click the plus and minus buttons to zoom in and out.

- Click the arrows in the view to move along the streets.

- Drag the view to rotate the line of sight and look up or down.

- Click the compass 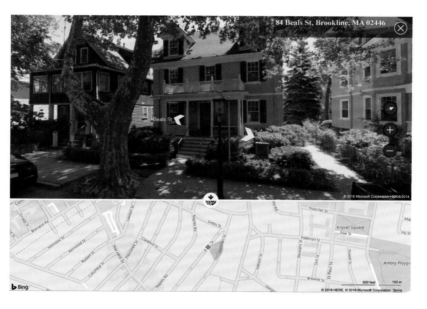 icon to reset the view to looking due north.

- Click the **Show location on a map** button to show the current Streetside location on a Road map. The location is marked by an orange diamond, and the field of vision is also shown. To jump to another location, drag the map so that the location you want comes under the orange diamond. To hide the Road map, click the **Hide map** button.

5. To leave Streetside view and return to the view you were in before entering Streetside (Road or Aerial), click the Close button in the top-right corner.

Finding Places of Interest

Family Tree Maker helps you search for places of interest such
as libraries and cemeteries near important places in your family
history. If you're planning a research trip, you can use the maps to
view all the cemeteries and churches in your ancestor's hometown.
You can also type in other attractions and sights—try searching for
"hotel", "park", or even "gas station".

1. Click the **Places** button on the main toolbar.

2. If you've already entered the location in your tree, click its
    name in the **Places** panel; otherwise, enter the location's name
    in the blank field above the map on the right.

3. Choose a location type (such as libraries) from the drop-down
    list and click **Go**. (You can also type in your own search term
    in the Location field.) Blue pushpins appear for each item that
    matches your search.

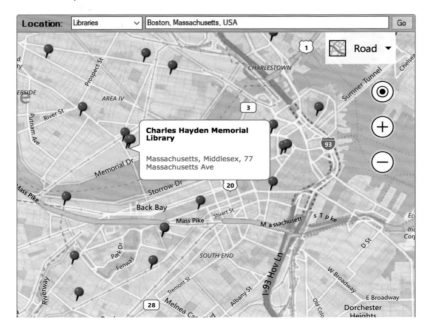

4. Move the pointer over a pushpin to see a name and address for the location (if available).

Printing a Map

You can print maps directly from the software, whether it's an aerial shot of your ancestor's farm or the migration path your great-grandfather took across the country.

1. On the Places workspace, access the map you want to print. The display window shows what part of the map will be printed. You may need to resize the workspace to display more of the map.

2. In the main toolbar, click the **Print** button and choose **Print Map** from the drop-down list. The Print window opens.

3. When prompted choose a printer, select the number of copies, and choose a page range.

4. Click **Print**.

Viewing Locations in Groups

On the Places workspace, you can view locations in an alphabetical list or grouped together by country, county, city, and so on. If you have hundreds of places in your tree, groups make it easier to quickly find the one you're interested in. An added benefit is that you can see all people who are associated with a specific country or city with one click.

Note: To make sure locations are grouped together correctly, you'll need to resolve any place name errors. For help, see "Standardizing Locations" on page 289.

1. In the Places workspace, click the **Alphabetical/Groups** button to toggle between showing places in an alphabetical list or by groups.

2. To see all places within a group, click its disclosure triangle. To expand all groups, click the **Expand All Nodes** button.

Viewing People and Facts Linked to a Location

Family Tree Maker lets you view all the events that took place at a
certain location and the people associated with each event.

1.   Click the **Places** button on the main toolbar.

2.   Click a location in the Places panel.

> Tip: If you're viewing locations in groups, you can see all the people
> and events for a group by clicking the **Linked to All** button and then
> clicking a country, state, or county in the list of places. Or view
> people and events just for a particular selected location by clicking
> the **Linked to This** button.

On the right side of the window, you'll see the selected location
and the individuals who have life events associated with it.

3.   Do one of the following:

     • To see the event that occurred at this location for a specific
       person, click the plus sign (+).

     • To see the events that occurred at this location for all the
       individuals, click the **Expand all items** button on the tool-
       bar and choose **Expand all**. (Click the **Collapse all items**
       button to close all the events.)

- To always have all people and events related to the selected location showing, click the **Expand** button on the toolbar and select **Expand All on Load**.

Creating Migration Maps

Maps can be extremely useful when tracing an ancestor. You can see at a glance all the locations that are connected with a specific individual or family, track migration patterns, and maybe discover where to locate more records.

Creating a Migration Map for an Individual

1. Click the **Places** button on the main toolbar. In the Places panel, choose "Person" from the **List by** drop-down list.

2. Click the individual whose migration map you want to see. A map appears in the display area; the individual's birthplace is indicated by a green marker and death place by a dark red marker.

To the right of the map is every fact you've entered for the individual—and its location.

3. Click the checkbox next to a fact to include its location in the migration map.

4. Position the pointer over a marker to see the location's name and the fact associated with it.

Creating a Migration Map for a Family

1. Click the **Places** button on the main toolbar. In the Places panel, choose "Person" from the **List by** drop-down list and click an individual.

2. To view the locations associated with the individual's immediate family (parents, siblings, spouse, and children), click the **Include immediate family** button in the mapping toolbar.

3. Click any individual's name to the right of the map to highlight his or her life events on the map. The migration path for the individual is indicated by a thick line.

    Tip: You can change the color of a migration path by clicking the line color buttons in the mapping toolbar.

4. To view locations associated with an individual's ancestors (up to four generations), click the **Ancestor generations** button in the mapping toolbar and choose the number of generations from the drop-down.

    A map appears in the display area: birthplaces are indicated by green markers and death places by dark red markers; the migration path for each individual is indicated by a colored line.

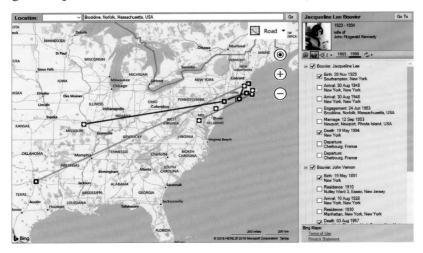

Entering GPS Coordinates

Although the online maps are able to recognize most places, there are times when it won't be able to identify a location. Perhaps your grandmother is buried in a rural cemetery or census records show your family in a township that no longer exists. You can set a location's exact position using GPS (Global Positioning System) coordinates.

1. Click the **Places** button on the main toolbar. In the Places panel, click the name of the location to which you want to add GPS coordinates.

2. Place your cursor in the **Location** field and then click the **Location calculator** 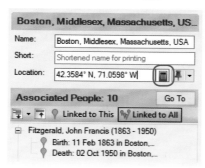 icon that appears.

The Location Calculator opens. You can enter the coordinates in degrees:minutes:seconds, degrees:decimal minutes, or decimal degrees.

3. Enter the coordinates for the location and click **OK**.

Entering a Display Name for a Location

Recording locations in a complete and consistent manner is an important part of creating a quality family history. Unfortunately, long location names can clutter your reports and charts. To avoid this problem, you can enter your own shortened or abbreviated display names. For example, instead of using Heidelberg, Baden-Württemberg, Germany, for a birthplace, you can enter Heidelberg, Germany, as the display name.

1. Click the **Places** button on the main toolbar. In the **Places** panel, choose "Place" from the **List by** drop-down list.

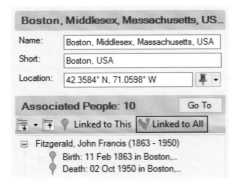

2. Click the name of the location you want to change.

3. Enter a display name in the **Short** field.

Chapter Eight
Researching Your Tree Online

As you enter stories and facts, you'll probably notice that more information about your family is waiting to be discovered—perhaps it's the burial location of your grandfather or the wedding certificate for your aunt and uncle. Family Tree Maker can help you fill in these gaps in your research with hints—behind-the-scenes searches of Ancestry and FamilySearch.

You can also search for information on RootsWeb.com or any of your favorite websites. If you find info that matches a family member, you can quickly add it to your tree—without leaving Family Tree Maker.

Ancestry Hints

Once your FTM tree is uploaded to Ancestry to create a linked Ancestry tree, Family Tree Maker automatically searches thousands of databases on Ancestry looking for information that matches people in your tree. When a possible match is found, a green leaf or "hint" appears next to an individual in the tree viewer and editing panel on the People workspace.

You can view the results when it's convenient, and if the information is relevant, you can add it to your tree.

FamilySearch Hints

FamilySearch, the largest genealogy organization in the world, is operated by The Church of Jesus Christ of Latter-day Saints.

Millions of people use FamilySearch records, resources, and services each year to learn more about their family history.

Family Tree Maker 2017 provides you with direct access to FamilySearch's Family Tree database of more than one billion names. You can get automatic match suggestions (hints), search the database, and merge any useful records you find into your own tree, just as you can with records you find on Ancestry's databases.

Note: If you don't want Family Tree Maker to automatically search Ancestry or FamilySearch when you're connected to the Internet, you can turn this feature off. To do this, choose **Tools>Options**, click **General** and deselect options for hints.

Viewing Ancestry and FamilySearch Hints

If Family Tree Maker finds records or trees on Ancestry or FamilySearch that might match an individual in your tree, you'll see a "hint" icon—a green leaf or a blue square respectively—next to the person on the People workspace. Move the pointer over the icon to see the number of records and trees that were found.

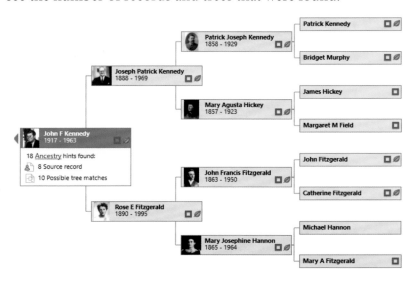

Note: To view Ancestry Hints you must have an Internet connection, log in to your Ancestry account, have your FTM tree linked to Ancestry tree, and — to get hints for new people you add to your tree — keep your FTM and Ancestry trees synced. To view the actual records and images, you must have an Ancestry subscription.

1. Go to the **Tree** tab on the People workspace. In the tree viewer or editing panel, click a hint icon.

2. Select a hint that interests you from the hint results list. If the record matches someone in your family, you can add it to your tree. (See "Adding Records to a Tree" on page 134.) If the record does not match anyone in your tree, you can ignore it. (See "Ignoring Hints" below.)

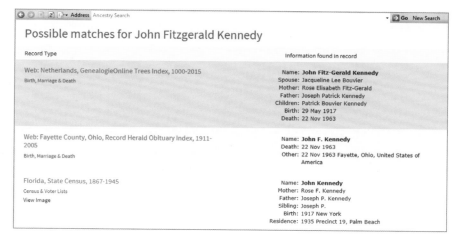

Ignoring Hints

If a hint is not relevant to someone in your tree, you can ignore it so it won't appear in your list of hints again.

1. Access the hints for an individual.

2. On the Possible Matches page, click the hint you want to ignore.

3. On the Search Result Detail toolbar, click the **Ignore record** icon (a circle with a diagonal line through it).

To indicate the hint has been ignored, the icon appears with a black box around it and an orange background.

Viewing Ignored Hints

If you've chosen to ignore specific hints for an individual, you can still view them at a later time.

1. Click the **Web Search** button on the main toolbar. Choose the individual whose hints you'd like to view.

2. Select Ancestry or FamilySearch in the Search Locations list.

3. Click **Search>View Ignored Records**. If the individual has no ignored hints, a corresponding message appears.

4. To take the hint off the Ignore list, click the **Ignore record** icon.

Searching Ancestry

You don't have to wait for Ancestry Hints to help you discover facts about your family, you can search the website any time you like.

Note: Although anyone can view Ancestry search results, you must have a subscription to view the actual records and images.

1. Click the **Web Search** button on the main toolbar.

2. Select **Ancestry** in the Search Locations list. If you want to research someone other than the individual who is currently selected, use the mini pedigree tree or the Index of Individuals button to choose the appropriate person.

    Notice that some fields have been filled in for you already.

    By some fields you'll see an **Exact** checkbox. Use these options to limit your results to records that match your search terms exactly. Start by entering just one or two search terms, such as name and location.

What Can I Find on Ancestry.com?

Ancestry.com is the world's largest online family history resource with more than 20 billion historical records—and more being added all the time. Here's a sample of the wealth of information available on Ancestry:

- A complete U.S. census collection (1790–1940). You'll also find census records for the UK, Australia, Canada, and other countries.
- Immigration records and passenger lists from 1820 to 1960.
- Birth, marriage, and death records back as far as the 16th century.
- More than 550 million military records from the 1600s to the Vietnam War and beyond.
- More than 150 million pages from historical newspapers as far back as the 1700s.
- More than 20,000 local histories, memoirs, journals, and biographies.
- Thousands of photos from the Library of Congress, maps beginning in the 1500s, and photographs dating back to the mid-1800s.
- Over 90 million family trees from all over the world—created by researchers just like you. Within these trees you'll find 330 million photographs, scanned documents, and stories.

3. Add or delete names, dates, and places as necessary.

4. To display records for a specific country or ethnicity first in your search results, choose an option from the **Collection Focus** drop-down list.

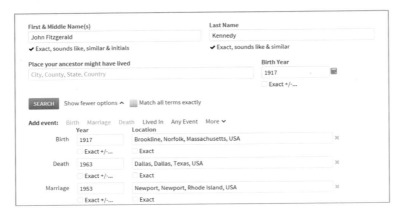

5. To limit your search results to a specific type of record:

   - Click the **Historical records** checkbox to search for birth records, censuses, military and immigration records, etc.

   - Click the **Stories & publications** checkbox to search for member-submitted stories, newspapers, and county histories.

   - Click the **Family Trees** checkbox to search trees submitted by members.

   - Click the **Photos and maps** checkbox to search maps, historical images, and member-submitted photos.

6. Click **Search**.

7. If you get a large number of search results or matches, click the **Edit Search** button to narrow your search. Try adding more dates, a gender, or a spouse's name. (You can also narrow your

search by clicking a category link at the top of the window.) If you get too few results or no matches, delete one or more of your search terms to broaden your search.

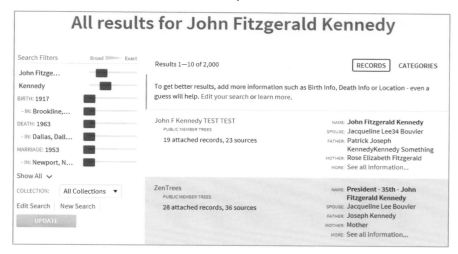

8. Click a search result to see the record or index. The tab at the bottom of the window lets you compare, side-by-side, the facts in your tree with the details found in the highlighted record.

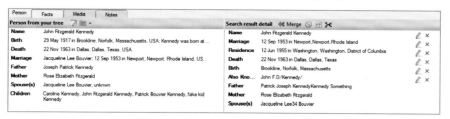

9. If the information matches what you already know about the individual and his or her family, you can add the information to your tree. (For instructions, see "Adding Records to a Tree" on page 134.)

Ancestry Search Tips

Ancestry automatically includes name variations, abbreviations, and nicknames when it searches for records. But if you're searching for an elusive ancestor, try these tips to get the most out of your searches:

- **Use wildcards.** Wildcards represent unknown letters in a name. Use an asterisk for up to six characters; a search for "fran*" will return results for Fran, Franny, Frank, Frannie, and Frankie; use a question mark for a single character; a search for "Hans?n" will return matches such as Hansen and Hanson.

- **Search for similar-sounding names.** You can search for last names that "sound like" the one you're looking for. For example, a search for Smith would return Smithe, Smyth, and Smythe. To do so, click the "Exact..." link under the individual's surname. Then click the **Sounds like**, **Soundex,** and **Similar** checkboxes.

- **Estimate dates.** Not sure of the exact date of an event? Make an educated guess; you'll get better results than if you leave the field blank.

- **Add multiple locations.** If a family member lived in New York, Pennsylvania, and Illinois, add each of these residences to your search and you'll get results for all locations at once. To do this, click the "Show more options" link at the bottom of the search page. Then add additional locations in the event location fields.

- **Narrow your search by content.** Search for a specific type of content, such as a family trees, historical records, or photo and maps. To do this, click the necessary checkboxes at the bottom of the search form.

- **Search in specific collections.** Ancestry has special collections focused on countries and ethnicities. If you're looking for an individual who lived in only one country, you can narrow your search to that location. Simply choose an option from the "Collection Focus" drop-down list.

FamilySearch Search Tips

- **Search for name variations.** Try searching for variations in spelling or different variations of the same name. You can also try nicknames, different middle names and abbreviations.

- **Use wildcards.** Wildcards allow you to replace letters in a person's name and check for multiple spellings in a single search. A question mark (?) replaces a single character, and an asterisk (*) replaces multiple characters. For example, searching for Sm?th will return results for Smith, Smeth, or even Smythe. A search for Joh* will find matches such as John, Johnson, or Johnathon.

- **Estimate dates.** Not sure of the exact date of an event? Make an educated guess; you might get better results than if you leave the field blank.

- **Provide less information.** Adding too much information to your search may exclude results that don't have all that information, or where some of the information differs. For example, try entering just a name and one event, or use only the name if it's not very common.

- **Provide more or different information.** Adding more information may help to find a record that matches more closely.

- **Use exact searching carefully.** Keep in mind that using the "Match All Exactly" checkbox returns fewer results. On the other hand, exact searching might be very helpful, limiting the results to people who lived in a specific place and time.

- **Use other alphabets.** If the person was from a country with a different alphabet, try looking for the name written in the person's native language.

Important: You can use the Find feature to find only deceased people in the FamilySearch Family Tree; you cannot look up living people.

Searching FamilySearch

You can search the FamilySearch Family Tree database without waiting for FamilySearch hints to appear. This will produce a list of possible matches to people in your tree. You can then review the possible matches and merge any information that you find to be relevant into your Family Tree Maker tree.

1.   Go to the **Web Search** workspace.

2.   In the Search Locations list, select **FamilySearch.org**.

3.   In the search form, enter information about an individual for whom you want to search.

4.   Click **Find**. The search results appear.

5.   Select a search result and look through the person's data in the **Search Results Detail** area. If this is the individual you were looking for, you can add the information you have found to your tree. (See "Adding Records to a Tree" below.)

Adding Records to a Tree

When you find a relevant record or family tree on Ancestry or FamilySearch, you can add the information directly to your tree using the Web Merge Wizard. You can choose the pieces of information you want to add and whether that information will be "preferred" or "alternate." The wizard can even include record images and sources for you automatically.

Note: It is always a good idea to save a backup of your tree file before making major changes using Web Merge.

1.   In the Web Search workspace, access the record that you want to add to your tree.

2. Make sure the individual you want to add the record to is
selected in the Person from Your Tree section. If you need to
merge the record with a different person, click the **Select a Different Person** button (a file folder icon) in the toolbar. Choose
an individual and click **OK**.

The bottom of the window displays the information in your
tree compared side-by-side with the information found in the
online record.

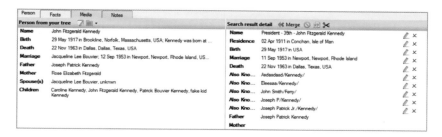

3. Click **Merge**. The Web Merge Wizard will launch. Depending
on the type of record you're accessing, the wizard may contain
multiple pages.

The left side of the window lists the names of the people
included in the record you are adding. As you move through
the wizard, each individual will be highlighted as you make
decisions about his or her information. Next to the individuals' names, you'll see two columns: the Person from My Tree
column shows the information you already have in your tree
and the Person from Web Search column shows the information from the record you are adding to your tree.

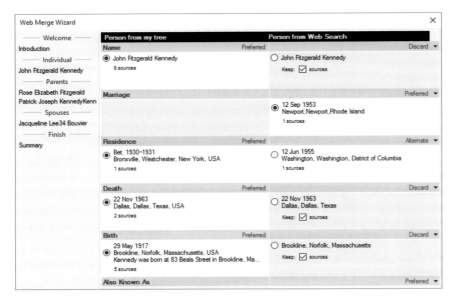

4. Use the buttons next to the facts in the two columns to determine how each fact will be added:

    •   To keep a fact and mark it as "preferred," select the button next to the fact. The corresponding fact for the other individual will be added as an alternate fact unless you choose to discard it.

    •   To remove a fact, click the arrow next to the Alternate heading and choose "Discard" from the drop-down list. This fact will not be added to your tree. Though you may choose to discard some facts for a person, it is usually a good idea to keep all facts in case they turn out to be relevant.

        If you discard a fact, you still have the option to add its source to your tree by clicking the **Keep sources** checkbox.

5. Click **Next** and do one of the following:

    •   If the individual you want to add has parents, spouse(s), or children associated with the record, the wizard asks if you want to add the information found for the first additional family member. Go on to step 6.

- If the individual doesn't have siblings or parents associated with the record, click the **Next** button to go to the Summary window. Skip to step 8.

6. Choose what you want to do with each family member. You can ignore the person, add the person as a new individual in your tree, or merge the person with an existing individual in your tree.

The details about the additional family members appear in the Person from Web Search column, while the information you already have in your tree appears in the Person from My Tree column. You can compare the information you have with what Family Tree Maker has found. If more than one individual appears in the Person from My Tree column, you will need to select the individual with whom you want to merge the new information.

7. Click **Next** and complete step 6 for every name in the record until all additional family members have been looked through. When you have made decisions for each family member, the Summary window opens.

8. Verify your selections in the Summary window. If you want to include an image of a record as a media item, click the **Media** checkbox. When you're ready, click **Merge Now**. A message tells you when the information has been successfully added to your tree. Click **Close** to close the message.

Note: You *cannot* undo a merge. However, if you decide you made a mistake, you can simply delete the fact(s) or source(s) that you added.

Searching Online with Family Tree Maker

With Family Tree Maker, you have a convenient starting point for researching and expanding your family history—without interrupting your work. You can explore the Web using any of your favorite search engines or genealogy websites. Then use the "Web clipping" tool to select text and images you're interested in and add them to individuals in your tree.

1. Click the **Web Search** button on the main toolbar. Using the mini pedigree tree or Index of Individuals button, choose the individual whose information you want to search for.

2. In **Search Locations**, click the website that you want to search, or enter a website in the **Address** field of the Web browser. The website opens.

3. Look for information on your ancestors just as you would if you were performing any kind of online search.

Copying Online Facts

If you find details on a website that you'd like to add to your tree, you can use the "Web clipping" tool. In some cases, Family Tree Maker will recognize the type of information you're viewing and will give you relevant fields to choose from. For example, if you add info from the Social Security Death Index, you'll have the option to add the text to a name, Social Security Number, birth fact, or death fact.

1. Access the website you want to copy facts from.

2. If you want to link the facts to a different person, click the **Select a different person** button in the **Person from Your Tree** section which is located at the bottom of the window. Select an individual and click **OK**.

3. Click the **Facts** tab at the bottom of the window. On the Search Result Detail toolbar, click the **Enable web clipping** icon.

4. Move the pointer over text on the website until the pointer turns into a cursor. Highlight the text you want to copy. A drop-down list appears.

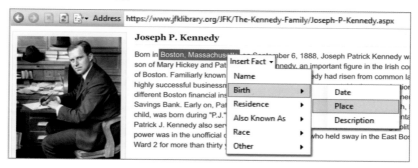

5. Choose a fact from the **Insert Fact** drop-down list. For example, you can choose the birthplace fact. The highlighted information now appears in the Search Result Detail section.

    Tip: You can copy multiple facts before adding the information to your tree; you don't need to add each fact individually.

6. When you have selected all the information you want, click **Merge**. The Web Merge Wizard will launch.

7. Use the buttons next to the facts in the two columns to determine how each fact will be added:

    •   To keep a fact and mark it as "preferred," select the button next to the fact. The corresponding fact for the other individual will be added as an alternate fact unless you discard it.

    •   To remove a fact, click the arrow next to the Alternate heading and choose "Discard" from the drop-down list. This fact will not be added to your tree. Though you may choose to discard some facts for a person, it is usually a good idea to keep all facts in case they turn out to be relevant.

        If you discard a fact, you still have the option to add its source to your tree by clicking the **Keep sources** checkbox.

8. Click **Summary** to see how the information will be added to your tree. If necessary, click **Edit** to enter a source citation for the information. (The default source citation is the URL, or Web address, where the information was found.)

9. Click **Merge Now**. A message tells you when the information has been added successfully. Click **Close** to close the message.

Copying an Online Image

You may find family photos or historical documents that will enhance your family history. Family Tree Maker makes it easy to add these directly from a website to your tree.

Note: Before copying any images from the Web, make sure you aren't violating any copyrights and/or get permission from the owner.

1. Access the Web page with the image you want to copy.

2. If you want to link the image to a different person, click the **Select a different person** button in the **Person from Your Tree** section which is located at the bottom of the window. Select an individual and click **OK**.

3. Click the **Media** tab at the bottom of the window. On the Search Result Detail toolbar, click the **Enable web clipping** icon.

4. Move the pointer over the Web page until the image you want is highlighted by a green dotted line.

5. Click the highlighted image. A thumbnail of the image appears in the Search Result Detail section.

6. When you have selected all the images you want, click **Merge**. A message tells you when the image has been added successfully. Click **Close** to close the message.

Note: The image will be linked to the person displayed in the Person from Your Tree section. You can also view it on the Media workspace.

Copying Online Text to a Note

While surfing the Web, you may come upon interesting stories about the founding of your grandfather's hometown or a description of the ship your great-grandparents sailed to America on. You can easily save this type of information using the "Web clipping" tool.

1. Access the website you want to copy text from.

2. If you want to link the notes to a person in your tree who is different from the currently selected individual, click the **Select a different person** button in the Person from Your Tree section. Choose an individual and click **OK**.

3. Click the **Notes** tab at the bottom of the window. To add the text as a personal note, click the **Person note** button; to add the text as a research note, click the **Research note** button.

4. On the Search Result Detail toolbar, click the **Enable web clipping** icon.

5. Move the pointer over text on the website until the pointer turns into a cursor. Highlight the text you want to copy. The **Insert note** button appears.

6. Click **Insert note**. The information now appears in the Search Result Detail section.

7. Click **Merge**. A message tells you when the text has been added successfully. Click **OK**.

Note: The note will be linked to the person in the Person from Your Tree section. To view the notes later, go to the individual's Person tab and click the Notes tab at the bottom of the window.

Archiving a Web Page

Websites are constantly changing and even disappearing. If you find a website you want to refer to multiple times, or if you find a site that contains too much information to read in one sitting, you might want to archive the Web page. That way, you can read the page's contents and continue your research when it's convenient for you—without being connected to the Internet. When you archive a Web page, Family Tree Maker will save a "snapshot" of the page in HTML format that can be opened in any Web browser.

1. Access the Web page you want to archive.

2. If you want to link the archived page to a person in your tree who is different from the currently selected individual, click the **Select a different person** button in the Person from Your Tree section. Choose an individual and click **OK**.

3. Click the **Facts**, **Media**, or **Notes** tab. In the Search Result Detail toolbar, click the **Create page archive** icon (a picture frame icon). A thumbnail of the page appears in the Search Result Detail section.

4. Click **Merge**. A message tells you when the archived Web page has been added successfully. Click **Close** to close the message, and then click **OK**.

   Note: The archived page will be linked to the person in the Person from Your Tree section. To view the archived page later, go to the Media workspace.

Managing Research Websites

You can create a list of favorite family history websites so they're easy to visit.

Adding a Website to Your Favorites List

1. Click the **Web Search** button on the main toolbar. In **Search Locations**, click the **New** button.

2. If you are currently accessing the website, click the **Use Current Site** button. If not, enter the address for the website in the **URL address** field.

3. Enter a name for the website in the **Favorite name** field. This can be any name that helps you identify the website.

4. Click **OK**. The new website now appears in your list of personal favorites.

Sorting Your Website Favorites List

If you've gathered quite a few favorite sites, you can sort the list so it appears in an order that's useful to you. For example, if you visit some websites daily, you can put them at the top of the list.

1. Click the **Web Search** button on the main toolbar. Click the
    Manage Favorites button at the bottom of the **Search Loca-
    tions** area. The **Manage Favorites** dialog appears.

2. To display the websites in alphabetical order, click **Sort favor-
    ites alphabetically**. To choose your own display order for the
    websites, click a website in the Personal favorites list and then
    click the up and down arrows. When you're finished, click **OK**.

Part Three

Creating Charts, Reports, and Books

Chapter Nine
Creating Family Tree Charts

After spending time gathering, compiling, and entering your family's history, it's time to show off your hard work. Family Tree Maker offers a wide variety of family tree charts to help you bring your family history to life. Add your own personal touch by customizing the charts with attractive backgrounds, colors, photos, fonts, and more. These charts help you quickly view the relationships between family members and are also a fun way to share your discoveries—hang a framed family tree in your home, print out multiple copies to share at a family reunion, or email charts to distant relatives.

As you begin creating your own charts, you might want to experiment with various formatting options, print out different versions, and see what you like best.

Pedigree Charts

The pedigree chart is a standard tool of genealogists and what most people think of when they hear the term "family tree." This chart shows the direct ancestors of one individual—parents, grandparents, great-grandparents, and so on.

Standard Pedigree Charts

In the standard pedigree chart (fig. 9-1), the primary individual is on the left side of the tree, with ancestors branching off to the right—paternal ancestors on top and maternal ancestors on bottom.

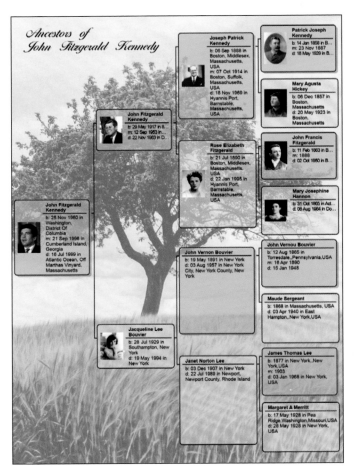

Figure 9-1. A pedigree chart using a custom template.

Vertical Pedigree Charts

In the vertical pedigree chart (fig. 9-2), the primary individual is shown at the bottom of the page, with his or her ancestors branching above the individual—paternal ancestors on the left and maternal ancestors on the right.

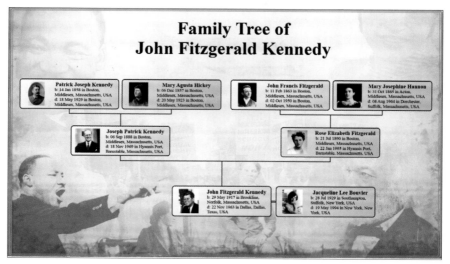

Figure 9-2. A customized vertical pedigree chart with portraits.

Hourglass Charts

An hourglass chart shows both the ancestors and descendants of an individual. The primary individual appears in the middle of the chart, with ancestors and descendants branching off in an hourglass shape.

Note: Because of its shape and the number of individuals included, most hourglass charts look best as posters.

Standard Hourglass Charts

In the standard hourglass chart, the primary individual appears in the middle of the chart, with ancestors branching above and descendants extending below the person.

Figure 9-3. An hourglass poster spread over six pages.

The chart in figure 9-3 shows an hourglass chart laid out as a poster. Notice the white spaces running vertically and horizontally across the pages. These show the margins of a standard 8½" by 11" sheet of paper. If you want to print the tree at home, you can use these guides to tape the pages together.

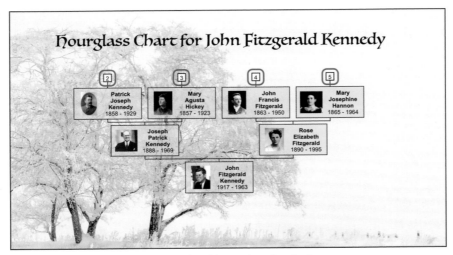

Figure 9-4. One page of a standard hourglass book chart.

You can also create standard hourglass charts that are useful for including in family history books. When you use the book layout, the chart is condensed into a series of individual family trees that appear on separate pages. The chart in figure 9-4 shows one page of a multi-page book-layout chart. Notice the numbered boxes in the upper part of the chart. When you are viewing the chart in Family Tree Maker, you can click one of these boxes to access that page of the chart. And when your chart is printed out, the numbered boxes help you navigate to related individuals found on other pages in the chart.

Horizontal Hourglass Charts

In the horizontal hourglass chart (fig. 9-5), the primary individual appears in the middle of the chart with ancestors branching to the right and descendants extending to the left of the person.

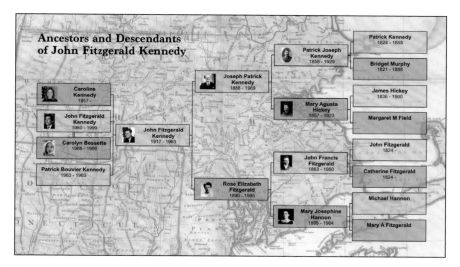

Figure 9-5. A horizontal hourglass chart.

Descendant Charts

The descendant chart shows the direct descendants of an individual—children, grandchildren, great-grandchildren, and so on. The primary individual is shown at the top of the chart, with descendants underneath in horizontal rows. You can also create a chart that shows the direct line between two selected individuals (fig. 9-6).

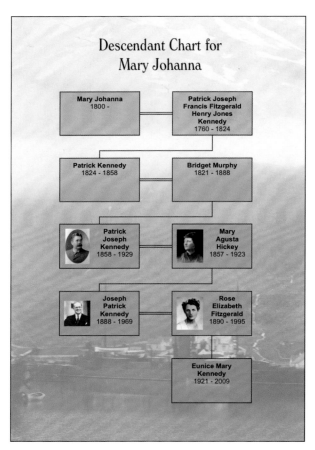

Figure 9-6. A direct-line descendant chart.

Bow Tie Charts

In the bow tie chart (fig. 9-7), the primary individual appears in the middle with paternal ancestors branching off to the left and maternal ancestors branching to the right.

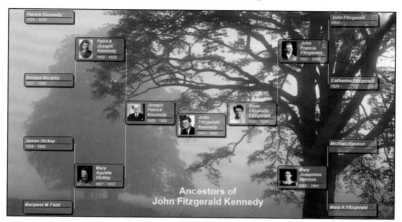

Figure 9-7. A customized bow tie chart.

Family Tree Charts

In the family tree chart (fig. 9-8), the primary individual appears at the bottom of the chart, with ancestors branching above him or her in a tree shape.

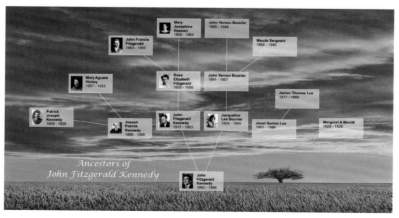

Figure 9-8. A customized family tree chart with images.

Fan Charts

A fan chart displays an individual's ancestors in a circular shape, one generation per level. The primary individual is at the center or bottom of the chart. You can choose between a full circle, semi-circle (fig. 9-9), quarter-circle, and more.

Figure 9-9. A customized semi-circle fan chart.

Note: Because of its shape and the number of individuals included, this chart is available only in poster layout.

Extended Family Charts

The extended family chart (fig. 9-10) can display every individual you've entered in your tree or just the people you select. The chart is arranged so that each generation appears on a separate horizontal row: children, parents, and grandparents, etc.

Note: Because of its shape and the number of individuals included, this chart is available only in poster layout.

Figure 9-10. A section of an extended family chart.

Relationship Charts

The relationship chart (fig. 9-11) is a graphical representation of one person's relationship to another. The common relative is shown at the top of the chart, with direct-line ancestors and descendants shown vertically beneath the individual.

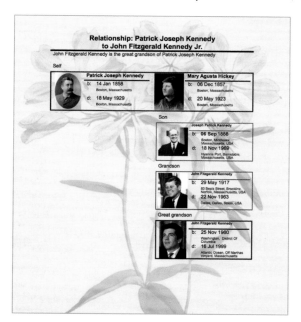

Figure 9-11. A relationship chart with a patterned background.

Creating a Chart

All charts are based on the last individual you were viewing in your tree. To change the primary individual in the chart, click his or her name in the mini pedigree tree above the chart, or click the Index of Individuals button and choose the person you want.

1. Go to the **Collection** tab on the Publish workspace. In **Publication Types**, click "Charts."

2. Double-click the chart icon, or select its icon then click the **Create Chart** button or the **Detail** tab.

3. Use the editing panel to change the chart.

Customizing a Chart

You can customize the contents and format of charts. For example, you can determine which facts are included and choose background images and fonts.

Note: You can save your custom changes as a template so you can use the same settings again. For instructions, see "Creating Your Own Template" on page 174.

Choosing Facts to Include in a Chart

In most charts you can choose which events or facts are included. Keep in mind, the more facts you add, the larger your chart will be.

1. Access the chart you want to change. In the editing toolbar, click the **Items to include** button.

The chart's default facts are shown in the Included facts list. You can add and delete facts and change their display options.

2. Do one of the following:

    •   To delete a fact, click the fact in the Included facts list and click the red (**X**) button.

    •   To add a fact, click the blue (+) button. The Select Fact window opens. Choose a fact from the list and click **OK**.

3. Change the fact options as necessary:

    •   **Include only preferred facts.** Click this checkbox to include only preferred facts. If you have multiple facts for the same event, only the preferred is included.

    •   **Include private facts.** Click this checkbox to include facts you've marked as private.

    •   **Include blank facts.** Click this checkbox to include a fact label even if the fact is empty.

    •   **Display user-defined short place name.** Click this check-box to use shortened place names for locations.

4. To change a fact's format, click the fact in the Included facts list and click the **[Fact Name] Options** button. Select the options you want and click **OK**.

Note: Options vary by fact. For example, you can include dates and locations in births, marriages, and deaths.

5. Click the **Print individual number with name** checkbox to assign numbers to individuals in the chart.

6. Click **OK**.

Changing a Chart's Title

You can change the title that appears at the top of a chart. Access the chart you want to change. In the editing panel, enter a new name in the **Chart title** field.

To reset the original chart title, click the button with a blue arrow on it.

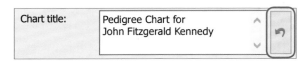

Including Source Information with a Chart

While you can't display sources in the actual chart, you can add a list of sources to the end of a chart (fig. 9-12).

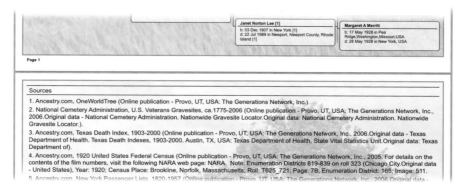

Figure 9-12. Sources for a pedigree chart.

1.   Access the chart you want to change. In the editing toolbar, click the **Items to include** button.

2.   Click the **Include sources** checkbox; then click **OK**.

Adding Images and Text to a Chart

You can personalize your charts and make them more appealing by adding backgrounds, family photographs and portraits, or stories.

Adding a Background Image

Family Tree Maker comes with hundreds of attractive images you can use as chart backgrounds. Or you can create a background using an image on your computer or a photo in your tree.

1.   Access the chart you want to change. In the editing panel, choose an image from the **Background** drop-down list:

   •   To use an image on your computer, click **Browse for Image**. Choose an image and click **Open**.

- To use an image in your tree, click **Select from Media Collection**. Choose an image and click **OK**.

2. Choose how the background will be displayed. To center the image on the page, choose **Center**. To stretch the image to fit the entire page, choose **Stretch**. To show a close-up of the image, choose **Zoom**. To show a series of the image, choose **Tile**.

3. Use the up and down arrows to set the intensity of the image. At 0 percent, the image will look normal, while a higher percentage will fade the image so the chart is easier to read.

Adding Portraits to a Chart

You can include images of individuals in a chart. In order to do this, you must have already added the images to your tree and linked them to specific individuals. (For instructions see "Adding a Portrait for an Individual" on page 96.)

1. Access the chart you want to change. Choose an image type from the **Pictures** drop-down list:

    • Choose **Thumbnail** to use low-resolution thumbnail images.

    • Choose **Photo** to use the resolution of the actual photo.

2. From the top drop-down list, choose how images are positioned next to fact boxes:

    • To align images with the middle of boxes, choose **Center**.

    • To align images with the top of boxes, choose **Top**.

    • To resize images to the same height as boxes, choose **Stretch**.

      Note: This option may cause your photos to look distorted.

    • To resize images to the same height as boxes (with cropped margins on the left and right side), choose **Zoom**.

3. From the bottom drop-down list, choose how images are displayed in fact boxes:

    • To display images on the left side, choose **Left**.

    • To display images on the right side, choose **Right**.

    • To display images as a background, choose **Behind**.

4. If you want to change the size of the photo or thumbnail, enter a size in the **Inches wide** field.

    Note: The larger the image is, the less space available for facts.

5. Click **Use silhouettes** to display a silhouette icon for individuals who don't have portraits.

Adding a Decorative Photo or Embellishment

You can add family photographs, borders, or embellishments to your charts.

1. Access the chart you want to change. In the editing toolbar, click the **Insert Image or Text Box** button.

2. Choose an image using the drop-down list:
    *   To use an image in your tree, click **Insert Image from Media Collection**. Choose an image and click **OK**.
    *   To use an image on your computer, click **Insert Image from File**. Choose an image and click **Open**.

    Note: You'll find a variety of decorative images in the Embellishments folder located in the Family Tree Maker folder.

3. To resize an image, click it. Then move the pointer over the icon in the bottom-right corner. Drag the image to the size you want.

4. To change the position of the image, move the pointer over the image and click and drag the image to the location you want.

Adding Text

You can add text anywhere on a chart. For example, you could write a short biography of the main person in the chart (fig. 9-13).

Figure 9-13. A family tree chart with a short biography.

1. Access the chart you want to add text to. In the editing toolbar, click the **Insert Image or Text Box** button.

2. Choose "Insert Text Box" from the drop-down list.

3. To change the position of the text box, move the pointer over the text. When the pointer changes shape, click and drag the box to the location you want.

4. To enter or edit text, simply double-click the box. Enter your text and click **OK**.

    Tip: To change the text's size or color, click the **Fonts** button in the charts toolbar. In "Items to format" select **Text Boxes**.

Changing the Header or Footer

You can define the headers and footers for each chart (the lines of text at the top and bottom of a chart).

Note: Not every option is available for every chart.

1. Access the chart you want to change. In the editing toolbar, click the **Header/Footer** button.

2. Change the header and footer options as necessary:

- **Chart note.** Enter any text you want to appear in the footer.

- **Draw box around footer.** Click this checkbox to enclose the footer in a box.

- **Print "Created with Family Tree Maker".** Click this checkbox to add this statement to the footer.

- **Include submitter info.** Click this checkbox to add your user information to the footer.

- **Include date of printing.** Click this checkbox to include the current date in the footer.

- **Include time of printing.** Click this checkbox to include the current time in the footer.

- **Include page/chart numbers.** Click this checkbox to include page numbers. From the drop-down list, choose whether the number appears in the header or footer.

  In **Starting number** enter the number of the chart's first page; in **Starting number for continuation charts**, enter the number of the second page of the chart.

3. Click **OK**.

Changing Formatting for a Chart

You can change a chart's formatting such as its fonts, colors and borders, and box sizes.

Changing Layout Options

Depending on the number of individuals and facts in your chart, you may need to adjust the layout and spacing to best display each individual.

Note: Not every option is available for every chart.

1. Access the chart you want to change. The editing panel displays the options you can change.

2.   Change the chart's layout options as necessary:

- **Layout.** Choose **Book** to create pages for a book; if a chart flows onto multiple pages, each page is cross-referenced to generations on other pages. Choose **Poster** to create pages that can be linked together to form a poster (click the **Advanced** button to customize the poster).

- **Overlap.** Change the horizontal spacing. Choose **No Overlap** to space columns equally; choose **Columns Overlap** to overlap columns slightly; choose **Only Root Overlaps** to overlap the primary individual's column with the parents' column; choose **FishTail** to overlap all columns except the last generation.

- **Spacing.** Change the vertical spacing. Choose **Perfect** to space rows evenly; choose **Collapsed** to space rows closer together; choose **Squished** to use minimal space between rows; choose **Custom** to adjust the spacing using the Advanced poster format.

    Tip: Collapse or squish columns if you want to fit many people on one page.

- **Align nodes.** Choose how lines connect individuals. Choose **Top** to use lines underneath names; choose **Center** to center lines next to each person; choose **Bezier** to use curved lines; choose **Straight** to use diagonal lines.

- **Center tree on page.** Click this checkbox to display the tree in the center of the page. If the chart is for a book, don't use this option. Instead, leave extra space in the left margin for binding.

- **Last descendant generation vertically.** Click this checkbox to show the last generation under their parents.

- **Boxes overlap page breaks.** Click this checkbox so boxes that fall on a page break will not be split over two pages.

- **Include empty branches.** In the Book layout, displays all branches of the tree through the generations you have specified even if there is no person entered for them.

  Printing empty branches is useful when you want to collect more information about your family. You can fill out the boxes by hand and later transfer the information into Family Tree Maker. In the Poster layout this option is available only for Pedigree and Fan charts.

- **Include duplicate ancestor lines.** If you have an instance of intermarriage in your family (for example, cousins marrying back into the family), you will have some duplicate individuals in your tree. Select this option if you want these individuals to print in your tree more than once.

- **Include siblings of primary individual.** Displays the brothers and sisters of the person selected for the chart. Siblings are displayed on the same level as the primary person. This option is not available in the Book layout.

- **Include spouses of primary individual.** Displays each husband or wife of the person selected for the chart. This option is not available in the Book layout for all charts.

- **Include all individuals.** Includes everyone entered in the tree file in the chart, even those individuals who may not be attached to the main tree. These unrelated people are displayed in a separate tree (or trees) at the bottom of the chart. When this option is not selected, unrelated people do not appear in the chart.

- **Display relationship label for each node.** Shows each person's relationship to the person in the "Relation from" field.

- **Show generation labels.** Displays the relationship of the generation (parent, grandparent, and so on) to primary person above each column of the chart (excluding the root). The font and box style can be configured for all generation labels by clicking the **Fonts** and the **Box and line styles** buttons in the editing toolbar.

  Note: You cannot move the generation labels. If you manually change the location of the columns, the labels may no longer be aligned.

- **Show thumbnail.** Displays the picture you assigned to each person that appears on the chart. If a picture is not available, a silhouette is displayed instead.

- **Include civil/canon information.** Displays the civil and canon degrees of separation at the bottom of the chart. For more information, see "Civil Degree" and "Canon Degree" in the Relationship Calculator section of Chapter 13 (page 250).

- **Root Node at Fan Origin.** Orients the primary person's box so that it is square with the page. In charts of 90 degrees or less, the primary person's node is placed in the bottom-left corner of the chart. When not selected, the root node is placed closer to the other nodes and oriented with the chart.

- **Fan layout.** Specifies the number of degrees to use for the chart. The dark portion of each circle indicates how the chart will appear.

Adding Page Borders, Text Boxes, and Background Colors

You can enhance a chart by adding a border, background color, and text boxes.

Note: Not every option is available for every chart.

1.   Access the chart you want to change. In the editing toolbar, click the **Box and line styles** button.

2.   To change the format of text boxes, click a group in the Boxes list.

3. Change these options as necessary:

    - Choose border, fill, and shadow colors from the drop-down lists.

    - Click **Double line** to add two lines to box borders.

    - Click **Rounded corners** to use round corners for box borders.

    - Click **Semi-transparent** to make the background image or color partially visible through boxes.

    - Click **Use gradient fill** to make a box's fill color go from light to dark.

    - Click **All boxes same size** to make all boxes on the chart the same size.

4. To change the size of boxes, enter the maximum width and height (in inches) for boxes in the "Book layout maximums."

5. To change the format of pedigree and divider lines, choose colors from the drop-down lists. Then choose the line thickness.

6. To add a border to the entire chart, choose a color from the **Line** drop-down list. Then click **Double line** to add two lines to the page border; click **Rounded corners** to use round corners for the page border.

7. To add a colored background, choose the color from the **Background** drop-down list. (Choose "None" for a blank background.)

8. Click **OK**.

Changing Fonts

You can change the appearance of the text in charts to make it more formal, more fun, or maybe just more readable.

1. Access the chart you want to change. In the editing toolbar, click the **Fonts** button.

2. In the Items to format list, click the text element, such as the chart title, you want to change.

3. Choose a font from the **Font** drop-down list. You can also change the size of the font, its style, color, and alignment.

4. Click **OK** to save your changes.

Using Chart Templates

Family Tree Maker comes with several templates you can use to quickly dress up your family tree charts. You can also turn your own chart designs into templates.

Creating Your Own Template

After you've customized a chart with your favorite fonts and colors and changed the spacing and layout to make everyone fit perfectly on the page, you don't want to lose your settings. You can save your modifications as a template, and you won't have to recreate your changes if you want to use them on another chart.

1. After you've modified a chart, click the **Save settings** 🛠 button in the editing toolbar.

2. Choose one of the following:

   • **Save as preferred template.** This option saves the current settings as the preferred template for all charts. However, this template isn't permanent; if you modify the preferred template, the old settings will be written over.

   • **Create new template.** This option lets you name the template and add it to the list of custom chart templates.

3. Click **OK**. To assign your template to a chart see the next section.

Using a Custom Template

Family Tree Maker lets you use attractive templates to instantly change the look of your chart.

You can apply custom templates to any chart. And if the results aren't exactly what you want, you can modify it.

1. Access the chart you want to apply a template to. Click the **Use saved settings** button in the editing toolbar.

2. Choose one of these template options:

    •   **Default template.** This is the default chart template.

    •   **Preferred template.** This is a template you have created and saved as your "preferred" template.

    •   **Custom template.** These are the custom templates found in Family Tree Maker (or templates you have created).

3. Click **OK**.

Saving Charts

You can save a specific chart in Family Tree Maker, or you can save a chart in different file formats to export.

Saving a Specific Chart

If you like a chart you've created, you'll probably want to save it. That way you can view it again without having to recreate it.

1. After you've modified a chart, click the **Save chart** button in the editing toolbar.

2. Enter a unique name for the chart. For example, don't use generic terms like "Pedigree Chart" or "Relationship Chart."

3. Click **Save**.

Tip: To open a saved chart, go to the Collection tab on the Publish work-space. In Publication Types, click **Saved Charts**. Then double-click the chart you want to open.

Saving a Chart as a File

You may want to save a chart as an image or PDF so you can share it easily with family or post it online.

1. Access the chart you want to save.

2. Click the **Share** button above the editing panel. From the drop-down list, choose one of the following:

   • **Export to PDF.** An Adobe PDF (Portable Document Format) is useful because it keeps the formatting you select. If you print a chart or send it to a relative, the chart will look exactly as you see it on your monitor. You can't change a PDF within Family Tree Maker, and you need Adobe Reader to view it. (Adobe Reader can be downloaded for free from the Adobe website.)

   • **Export to One Page PDF.** This option exports the chart as one page (regardless of size). Use this option if you're creating a poster-sized chart or printing a chart at a copy store.

   • **Export to Image.** This option lets you create an image of the chart as a bitmap, JPEG, or other image format.

   Each format has its own export options. After you choose a format type, you may be able to choose options such as page borders. Once you've made your selections, click **OK**.

3. Navigate to the location where you want to save the chart; then enter a name for the chart and click **Save**.

Printing a Chart

1. Access the chart you want to print.

2. Click the **Print** button above the editing panel.

3. When prompted choose a printer, select the number of copies, and choose a page range.

4. Click **OK**.

Sharing a Chart

You can share your charts with others by emailing them as PDFs.

Note: You must be connected to the Internet and have a desktop email program to use this feature.

1. Access the chart you want to email.

2. Click the **Share** button above the editing panel. From the drop-down list, choose **Send as PDF**.

3. Use the preview window to make sure the chart looks correct; then click **Send as PDF**.

4. Change any options as necessary and click **OK**.

5. Navigate to the location where you want to save the chart. Then enter a name for the chart and click **Save**. Family Tree Maker opens an email (with the file attached).

6. Send the email as you would any other.

Large Chart Printing

With Family Tree Maker, you can order a large, high-quality, professional print of your chart from the Family ChartMasters website in just a few clicks.

1. Access the chart you want to print.

2. Click the **Share** button above the editing panel, and then choose **Order Large Print at Family ChartMasters** from the drop-down list.

3. In the message that appears, click **Export Chart to PDF**.

4. Change any options as necessary, click **OK**, and then choose a location and click **Save**.

5. When the export process is complete, a new message appears. Click the **Go to Family ChartMasters** button.

6. The Family ChartMasters website opens in your default web browser. Follow the onscreen instructions to upload the exported file and order a large format print of your family tree.

Charting Companion Plug-In

If you like making charts with Family Tree Maker, you'll love the amazing array of additional chart types and settings you get with Progeny Genealogy's Charting Companion.

You can access the plug-in from the Tools menu and it will work directly with your charts as though it were part of Family Tree Maker.

Charting Companion provides six unique chart types not found in Family Tree Maker, including the Descendant Fan (a combination of descendant and family tree fan charts), plus a great collection of embellishments, and lots of special options for printing.

To get the plug-in, please visit www.familytreemaker.com and follow the **GIFT Collection** link.

Chapter Ten
Running Reports

Family Tree Maker includes a number of reports to help you organize and understand the information you've entered in your tree. You can create detailed reports about a single family, such as the family group sheet; relationship reports that show marriage events; bibliographies and source reports that help you keep track of your research; and more.

Each report can be customized—options differ by report. You can change fonts, add background images, and add headers and footers.

Genealogy Reports

Genealogy reports are a staple of serious family historians. These narrative reports contain biographical details about individuals. Relationships between people are shown using numbering systems that are unique to each report. You can choose from ancestor-ordered reports (Ahnentafels) or descendant-ordered reports.

Ahnentafel Report

The Ahnentafel (a German word meaning "ancestor table") is a numbered list of individuals (fig. 10-1). Its format is ancestor-ordered, meaning that it starts with one individual and moves backward in time to that individual's ancestors. This type of report isn't used frequently because it shows two family lines at the same time.

Figure 10-1. An Ahnentafel (ancestor report).

Descendant Report

A descendant report (fig. 10-2) is a narrative report that includes biographical information about each individual. It is descendant-ordered, meaning it starts with an individual and moves forward in time through that individual's children and grandchildren. You have four numbering system options: Register, NGSQ, Henry, and d'Aboville.

Figure 10-2. A Register descendant report.

Person Reports

Person reports give you an overview of your tree and help you focus on specific individuals.

Custom Report

Custom reports (fig. 10-3) let you explore your tree in ways that are interesting to you. For example, you can create a custom report of birthplaces or causes of death.

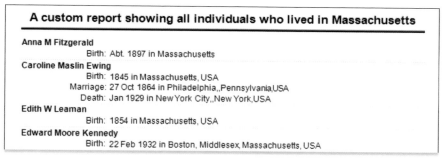

A custom report showing all individuals who lived in Massachusetts

Anna M Fitzgerald
        Birth: Abt. 1897 in Massachusetts
Caroline Maslin Ewing
        Birth: 1845 in Massachusetts, USA
        Marriage: 27 Oct 1864 in Philadelphia,,Pennsylvania,USA
        Death: Jan 1929 in New York City,,New York,USA
Edith W Leaman
        Birth: 1854 in Massachusetts, USA
Edward Moore Kennedy
        Birth: 22 Feb 1932 in Boston, Middlesex, Massachusetts, USA

Figure 10-3. A custom report of all individuals who lived in Massachusetts.

Data Errors Report

The Data Errors Report (fig. 10-4) lists all instances where data is missing or may be incorrect. This includes nonsensical dates (e.g., an individual being born before his or her parents were born), empty fields, and duplicate individuals. (For more information see "Running the Data Errors Report" on page 287.)

Data Errors Report		
Name	Birth Date	Potential Error
Bennett, Virginia Joan		The birth date is missing.
Bouvier, Jacqueline Lee	28 Nov 1929	Possible duplicate event Arrival Possible duplicate event Departure
Fitzgerald, Catherine	Abt. 1824	The individual has the same last name as his/her spouse, John Fitzgerald. The marriage date is missing.

Figure 10-4. A Data Errors Report.

Individual Report

The Individual Report (fig. 10-5) lists every fact and source you have recorded for a specific individual.

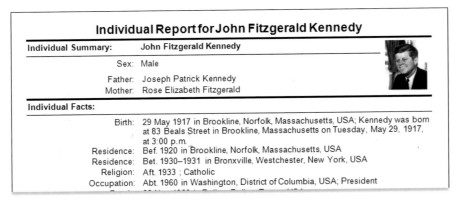

Figure 10-5. An Individual Report.

LDS Ordinances Report

The LDS Ordinances Report (fig. 10-6) is useful for members of The Church of Jesus Christ of Latter-day Saints and displays LDS-specific ordinances such as baptisms and sealings.

Figure 10-6. An LDS Ordinances Report.

LDS Ordinance Summary Report

The LDS Ordinance Summary Report (fig. 10-7) lists all people in the tree and their LDS ordinances status. You can restrict the report to selected individuals.

LDS Ordinance Summary

Name	Lifespan	Spouse	B	C	I	E	P	S
Field, Abraham	1870 - 1945	Jackson, Samantha	X			X		
Jackson, Samantha	1869 - 1934	Field, Abraham	X					X
Lawford, Thomas	1851 - Unknown	[unknown spouse]			X			
Smith, Herbert	Unknown - Unknown	Stewart, Phoebe Jackson						
Stewart, Phoebe Jackson	1900 - 1948	Smith, Herbert					X	

Figure 10-7. An LDS Ordinance Summary Report.

Note: Click **Tools > Options** and then select the **Show LDS information** checkbox to access the LDS Ordinances Report and the LDS Ordinance Summary Report.

List of Individuals Report

The List of Individuals Report has five options: all individuals in your tree, all individuals and their ID numbers, a list of anniversaries, a list of birthdays (fig. 10-8), and a contact list.

Birthday List

Name	Birth	Birthday
Schlossberg, Edwin	19 Jul 1945	72
Kennedy, Caroline	27 Nov 1957	60
Fitzgerald, Anna M	Abt. 1897	121
Fitzgerald, Katharine L	Abt. 1899	119

Figure 10-8. A list of birthdays.

Notes Report

The Notes Report (fig. 10-9) lets you view the person, research, relationship, or fact notes you've entered in your tree.

Notes Report

Fitzgerald, Rose Elizabeth	**21 Jul 1890 - 22 Jan 1995**
Person Note:	Year: 1920; Census Place: Brookline, Norfolk, Massachusetts; Roll: T625_721; Page: 7B; Enumeration District: 165; Image: 511.
	Year: 1900; Census Place: Boston Ward 6, Suffolk, Massachusetts; Roll: ; Page: ; Enumeration District: .
Kennedy, John Fitzgerald	**29 May 1917 - 22 Nov 1963**
Person Note:	Year: 1930; Census Place: Bronxville, Westchester, New York; Roll: 1659; Page: 2A; Enumeration District: 120; Image: 675.0.
Kennedy, Joseph Patrick	**09 Jun 1888 - 18 Nov 1969**
Person Note:	Year: 1938; Arrival: , ; Microfilm serial: T715; Microfilm roll: T715_6261; Line: ; List number:

Figure 10-9. A report of research notes.

Surname Report

The Surname Report (fig. 10-10) lists the total number of individuals with a specific surname, the number of males and females with that surname, and the earliest and most recent year a surname appears in your tree.

Surname Report

Surname	Count	Male	Female	Earliest	Most recent
Bennett	1	0	1		
Bouvier	1	0	1	1929	1929
Fitzgerald	8	3	5	1824	1899
Hannon	1	0	1	1865	1865
Kennedy	10	5	5	1888	1932
Lawford	1	1	0	1923	1923
Reggie	1	0	1		
Shriver	1	1	0	1916	1916
Skakel	1	0	1	1928	1928
Smith	1	1	0	1927	1927

Figure 10-10. A Surname Report sorted by name count.

Task List

A task list (fig. 10-11) displays all research tasks on your to-do list. You can see each task's priority, category, and creation and due dates.

Task List

Status	Task Information	Date Due
☐ ❗	Get military tree printed for Ramon Shanty Task for: General Task Categories: Created: 7/18/2017	
☐ ⊖	Check new DNA matches Task for: General Task Categories: Created: 7/18/2017	
☐ ⊖	Scan GrandPa Pete's journal Task for: General Task Categories: Created: 7/18/2017	

Figure 10-11. A research to-do list.

Timeline Report

A timeline (fig. 10-12) lists an individual's life events with the date and location of the event and the person's age at the time. You can also include events for an individual's immediate family (such as birth, marriage, and death) and historical events.

Timeline Report for John Francis Fitzgerald

	Yr/Age	Event	Date/Place/Description
	1863	Birth	11 Feb 1863 Boston, Middlesex, Massachusetts, USA
	1865 2	Birth (Spouse) Mary Josephine Hannon	31 Oct 1865 Acton, Middlesex, Massachusetts, USA
	1880 16	Residence	1880 Boston, Suffolk, Massachusetts, USA
	1888 24	Marriage Mary Josephine Hannon	1888
	1890 27	Birth (Daughter) Rose Elizabeth Fitzgerald	21 Jul 1890 Boston, Middlesex, Massachusetts, USA

Figure 10-12. A timeline for an individual and his family.

Relationship Reports

Relationship reports are just what they sound like; they show the relationships between different individuals and families in your tree.

Family Group Sheet

A family group sheet (fig. 10-13) is one of the most commonly used reports in family history. It is a detailed report about a single family (primarily the parents and children of a family, although it also includes the names of the couple's parents); including names, birth, death, and marriage information; notes; and sources. If the individual has more than one spouse, additional family group sheets will be created for each family.

Family Group Sheet for John Francis Fitzgerald

Husband:		John Francis Fitzgerald
	Birth:	11 Feb 1863 in Boston, Middlesex, Massachusetts, USA
	Marriage:	1888
	Death:	02 Oct 1950 in Boston, Middlesex, Massachusetts, USA
	Father:	John Fitzgerald
	Mother:	Catherine Fitzgerald
Wife:		Mary Josephine Hannon
	Birth:	31 Oct 1865 in Acton, Middlesex, Massachusetts, USA
	Death:	08 Aug 1964 in Dorchester, Suffolk, Massachusetts, USA
	Father:	
	Mother:	
Children:		
1 F	Name:	Rose Elizabeth Fitzgerald
	Birth:	21 Jul 1890 in Boston, Middlesex, Massachusetts, USA
	Marriage:	07 Oct 1914 in Boston, Suffolk, Massachusetts, USA
	Death:	22 Jan 1995 in Hyannis Port, Barnstable, Massachusetts, USA
	Spouse:	Joseph Patrick Kennedy

Figure 10-13. A family group sheet.

Kinship Report

The Kinship Report (fig. 10-14) helps you determine how individuals in your tree are related to a specific person.

Kinship Report for John Francis Fitzgerald		
Name:	**Birth Date:**	**Relationship:**
Bennett, Virginia Joan		Wife of grandson
Bouvier, Jacqueline Lee	28 Nov 1929	Wife of grandson
Fitzgerald, Anna M	Abt. 1897	Daughter
Fitzgerald, Catherine	Abt. 1824	Mother
Fitzgerald, Frances E	Abt. 1896	Daughter
Fitzgerald, George F	Abt. 1894	Son
Fitzgerald, John	Abt. 1824	Father
Fitzgerald, John Francis	11 Feb 1863	Self
Fitzgerald, Katharine L	Abt. 1899	Daughter
Fitzgerald, Rose Elizabeth	21 Jul 1890	Daughter
Hannon, Mary Josephine	31 Oct 1865	Wife

Figure 10-14. A Kinship Report.

Marriage Report

The Marriage Report (fig. 10-15) shows husbands and wives, their marriage dates, and relationship statuses.

Marriage Report			
Husband:	**Wife:**	**Marriage Date:**	**Relation:**
Cavendish, William	Kennedy, Kathleen "Kick" Agnes	06 May 1944	Spouse - Ongoing
Hickey, James			
Kennedy, Edward Moore	Bennett, Virginia Joan	29 Nov 1958	Spouse - Ongoing
Kennedy, Edward Moore	Reggie, Living		Spouse - Ongoing
Kennedy, John Fitzgerald	Bouvier, Jacqueline Lee	12 Sep 1953	Spouse - Ongoing
Kennedy, John Fitzgerald	Bessette, Carolyn	21 Sep 1996	Spouse - Ongoing
Kennedy, Joseph Patrick	Fitzgerald, Rose	07 Oct 1914	Spouse - Ongoing

Figure 10-15. A Marriage Report.

Outline Ancestor Report

The Outline Ancestor Report (fig. 10-16) shows where everyone fits in the family. Starting with a relative, it moves to the past, showing the primary individual's parents, grandparents, great-grandparents, and so on, generation by generation in outline format, with each individual on a separate line.

Outline Ancestor Report for Rose Elizabeth Fitzgerald

1 Rose Elizabeth Fitzgerald b: 21 Jul 1890 in Boston, Middlesex, Massachusetts, USA, d: 22 Jan 1995 in Hyannis Port, Barnstable, Massachusetts, USA
+ Joseph Patrick Kennedy b: 09 Jun 1888 in Boston, Middlesex, Massachusetts, USA, m: 07 Oct 1914 in Boston, Suffolk, Massachusetts, USA, d: 18 Nov 1969 in Hyannis Port, Barnstable, Massachusetts, USA
...2 John Francis Fitzgerald b: 11 Feb 1863 in Boston, Middlesex, Massachusetts, USA, d: 02 Oct 1950 in Boston, Middlesex, Massachusetts, USA
+ Mary Josephine Hannon b: 31 Oct 1865 in Acton, Middlesex, Massachusetts, USA, m: 1888, d: 08 Aug 1964 in Dorchester, Suffolk, Massachusetts, USA
......3 John Fitzgerald b: Abt. 1824 in Ireland
+ Catherine Fitzgerald b: Abt. 1824 in Ireland
......3 Catherine Fitzgerald b: Abt. 1824 in Ireland
+ John Fitzgerald b: Abt. 1824 in Ireland

Figure 10-16. An Outline Ancestor Report.

Outline Descendant Report

The Outline Descendant Report (fig. 10-17) starts with an ancestor and outlines each generation of descendants; you can choose the number of generations to show in the report.

Outline Descendant Report for John Francis Fitzgerald

1 John Francis Fitzgerald b: 11 Feb 1863 in Boston, Middlesex, Massachusetts, USA, d: 02 Oct 1950 in Boston, Middlesex, Massachusetts, USA
+ Mary Josephine Hannon b: 31 Oct 1865 in Acton, Middlesex, Massachusetts, USA, m: 1888, d: 08 Aug 1964 in Dorchester, Suffolk, Massachusetts, USA
...2 Rose Elizabeth Fitzgerald b: 21 Jul 1890 in Boston, Middlesex, Massachusetts, USA, d: 22 Jan 1995 in Hyannis Port, Barnstable, Massachusetts, USA
+ Joseph Patrick Kennedy b: 09 Jun 1888 in Boston, Middlesex, Massachusetts, USA, m: 07 Oct 1914 in Boston, Suffolk, Massachusetts, USA, d: 18 Nov 1969 in Hyannis Port, Barnstable, Massachusetts, USA
......3 Edward Moore Kennedy b: 22 Feb 1932 in Boston, Middlesex, Massachusetts, USA, d: 26 Aug 2009 in Hyannis Port, Barnstable, Massachusetts, USA
+ Virginia Joan Bennett m: 29 Nov 1958 in Bronxville, Westchester, New York, USA
.........4 Kara Anne Kennedy

Figure 10-17. An Outline Descendant Report.

Parentage Report

The Parentage Report (fig. 10-18) lists each individual, his or her parents, and their relationship (e.g., biological, adopted, foster).

Parentage Report		
Name	**Parents**	**Relationship**
Fitzgerald, Rose Elizabeth	Fitzgerald, John Francis	Biological
	Hannon, Mary Josephine	Biological
Kennedy, Joseph Patrick	Kennedy, Patrick Joseph	Biological
	Hickey, Mary Agusta	Biological
Kennedy, Edward Moore	Kennedy, Joseph Patrick	Biological
	Fitzgerald, Rose Elizabeth	Biological
Bennett, Virginia Joan		
Kennedy, Kara Anne	Kennedy, Edward Moore	Biological
	Bennett, Virginia Joan	Biological

Figure 10-18. A Parentage Report.

Family View Report

The Family View Report (fig. 10-19) shows three generations of ancestors for an individual and his or her parents and children.

Figure 10-19. A Family View Report.

Place Usage Report

The Place Usage Report (fig. 10-20) lists the locations in your tree and each person associated with them. You can also include specific events, such as birth or marriage, that occurred at that location.

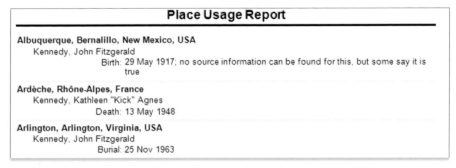

Figure 10-20. A Place Usage Report.

Media Reports

Media reports let you view items individually or in groups.

Photo Album

A photo album (fig. 10-21) shows a person's birth and death dates, the names of their parents, and all photos linked to them.

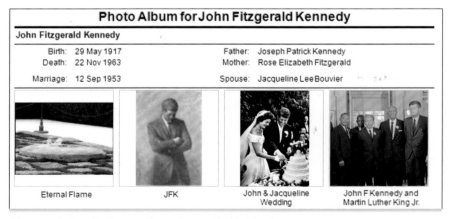

Figure 10-21. A photo album for an individual.

Media Item Report

A Media Item Report (fig. 10-22) shows an image (or icon) of a media item, its caption, date of origin, description, and the people the item is linked to.

Figure 10-22. A Media Item Report.

Media Usage Report

The Media Usage Report (fig. 10-23) lists all your media items. For each item you'll see a thumbnail, name, location on your computer, and people it is linked to.

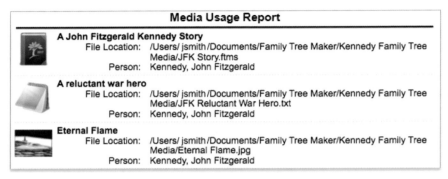

Figure 10-23. A Media Usage Report.

Source Reports

Family Tree Maker includes several reports that help you see how you've sourced facts in your tree.

Source Bibliography

A bibliography (fig. 10-24) is a detailed list of all the sources used in your research.

Source Bibliography
1860 United States Federal Census
1880 United States Federal Census
1900 United States Federal Census
1910 United States Federal Census
1920 United States Federal Census
1920 United States Federal Census
1930 United States Federal Census

Figure 10-24. An annotated bibliography.

Documented Facts Report

The Documented Facts Report (fig. 10-25) shows an individual and the events you've entered source information for.

Documented Facts

Bessette, Carolyn
Birth: 07 Jan 1966 in White Plains, Westchester, New York, USA
1 Ancestry.com, OneWorldTree (Online publication - Provo, UT, USA: The Generations Network, Inc.).
2 Ancestry.com, Massachusetts Death Index, 1970-2003 (Online publication - Provo, UT, USA: The Generations Network, Inc., 2005.Original data - State of Massachusetts. Massachusetts Death Index, 1970-2003. Boston, MA, USA: Commonwealth of Massachusetts Department of Health Services, 2005.Original data: State o).
3 Ancestry.com, Massachusetts Death Index, 1970-2003 (Online publication - Provo, UT, USA: The Generations Network, Inc., 2005.Original data - State of Massachusetts. Massachusetts Death Index, 1970-2003. Boston, MA, USA: Commonwealth of Massachusetts Department of Health Services, 2005.Original data: State o).
Death: 16 Jul 1999 in Massachusetts, USA
1 Ancestry.com, OneWorldTree (Online publication - Provo, UT, USA: The Generations Network, Inc.).
2 Ancestry.com, Massachusetts Death Index, 1970-2003 (Online publication - Provo, UT, USA: The Generations Network, Inc., 2005.Original data - State of Massachusetts.

Figure 10-25. A Documented Facts Report.

Undocumented Facts Report

The Undocumented Facts Report (fig. 10-26) shows individuals and events that don't have sources associated with them.

Undocumented Facts

Bennett, Virginia Joan
Marr: (Edward Moore Kennedy) 29 Nov 1958 in Bronxville, Westchester, New York, USA
Name: Bennett, Virginia Joan
Sex: Female

Bessette, Carolyn
Marr: (John Fitzgerald Kennedy) 21 Sep 1996 in Cumberland Island, Camden, Georgia, USA
Sex: Female

Bouvier, Jacqueline Lee
Engage: (John Fitzgerald Kennedy) 24 Jun 1953 in Brookline, Norfolk, Massachusetts, USA; John proposed to Jackie with a Van Cleef and Arpels engagement ring that his father helped him pick. The ring consisted of a 2.88 carat diamond and 2.84 carat emerald with tapering baguettes.
Sex: Female

Fitzgerald, Anna M
Sex: Female

Figure 10-26. An Undocumented Facts Report.

Source Usage Report

The Source Usage Report (fig. 10-27) shows each source and the individuals and facts associated with it.

Source Usage Report	

Source Title: [no source title]

Citation: Year: 1920; Census Place: Billington, Adams, Washington; Roll: T625_1920; Page: 1A; Enumeration District: 2; Image: 16.

Shriver, Robert Sargent

      Res: 1920 in Westminster, Carroll, Maryland, USA

      Birth: Abt. 1916 in Maryland, USA

      Name: Shriver, Robert Sargent

Source Title: **1860 United States Federal Census**

Citation: Ancestry.com, 1860 United States Federal Census (Online publication - Provo, UT, USA: The Generations Network, Inc., 2004. Original data - United States of America, Bureau of the Census. Eighth Census of the United States, 1860. Washington, D.C.: National Archives and Records Administration, 1860. M653, 1), Year: 1860; Census Place: Milford, Worcester, Massachusetts; Roll: M653_529; Page: 99; Image: 101. [Source citation includes media item(s)]

Figure 10-27. A Source Usage Report.

Calendars

You can make calendars (fig. 10-28) that display birthdays, death dates, and anniversaries for your immediate family or ancestors.

Figure 10-28. A calendar showing birth dates for all individuals.

Creating a Report

All reports are based on the last individual you were viewing in your tree. To change the primary individual in the report, click his or her name in the mini pedigree tree above the report, or click the Index of Individuals button and choose the person you want.

1.   Go to the **Collection** tab on the Publish workspace. In **Publication Types**, click the report type you want.

2.   Double-click the report icon, or select its icon and then click the **Create Report** button or the **Detail** tab.

3.   Use the editing panel to change the report.

Customizing a Report

You can customize the contents and format of reports. For example, you can determine which individuals and facts are included in the report and choose background images and fonts.

Choosing Facts to Include in a Report

In some reports you can choose which events or facts you'd like to include.

1.   Access the report you want to change. In the editing toolbar, click the **Items to include** button.

The Items to Include window opens. The report's default facts are shown in the Included facts list. You can add and delete facts and change their display options.

2. Do one of the following:

    • To delete a fact, click the fact in the Included facts list and click the red (**X**) button.

    • To add a fact, click the Add (+) button. The Select Fact window opens. Choose a fact from the list and click **OK**.

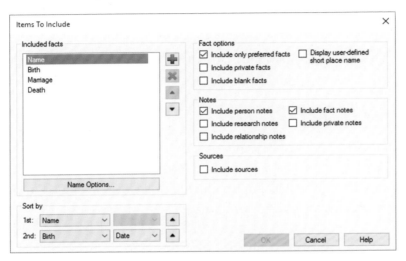

3. Change the fact options as necessary:

    • **Include only preferred facts.** Click this checkbox to include only preferred facts. If you have multiple facts for the same event, only the preferred one is included.

    • **Include private facts.** Click this checkbox to include facts you've marked as private.

    • **Include blank facts.** Click this checkbox to include a fact label even if the fact is empty.

    • **Display user-defined short place name.** Click this checkbox to use shortened place names for locations.

4. To change a fact's format, click the fact in the Included facts list and click the **Options** button. Select the options you want and click **OK**.

Note: Options vary by fact. For example, you can include dates and locations in births, marriages, and deaths.

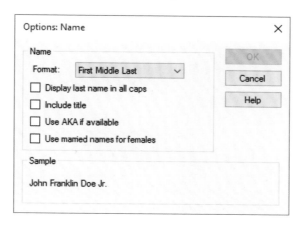

5. Choose notes to include in the report:

- Click **Include person notes** to show person notes linked to individuals.

- Click **Include research notes** to show research notes linked to individuals.

- Click **Include relationship notes** to show person notes linked to relationships.

- Click **Include fact notes** to show notes linked to facts.

- Click **Include private notes** to show a note even if it has been marked as private.

6. To show sources in the report, click the **Include sources** checkbox.

7. Click **OK**.

Choosing Individuals to Include in a Report

In many reports, you can choose which individuals will be included. For example, you can choose a specific ancestor and his or her descendants. You can also choose individuals by picking specific criteria (for example, you may want to generate a report that shows all individuals who were born in a particular city).

1. Access the report you want to change. You can choose individuals for the report in the editing panel.

2. Do one of the following:

   • To include the individual's immediate family members, click **Immediate family**.

   • To include also grandparents, aunts, uncles, first cousins, nieces, nephews, grandchildren, and spouses of all those who are listed, click **Extended family**.

   • To include everyone in your tree, click **All individuals**.

   • To choose specific individuals, click **Selected individuals**. The Filter Individuals window opens. Click a name and then click **Include** to add the person. When you're finished choosing individuals click **Apply**.

Changing a Report's Title

You can change the title that appears at the top of a report. Access the report you want to change. In the editing panel, enter a new name in the **Report title** field. Click the button next to this field to revert to the original report title.

Adding a Background Image

Family Tree Maker comes with hundreds of attractive images you can use as report backgrounds. Or you can create a background using an image on your computer or a photo in your tree.

1. Access the report you want to change. In the editing panel, choose an image from the **Background** drop-down list:

    •   To use an image on your computer, click **Browse for Image**. Choose an image and click **Open**.

    •   To use an image in your tree, click **Select from Media Collection**. Choose an image and click **OK**.

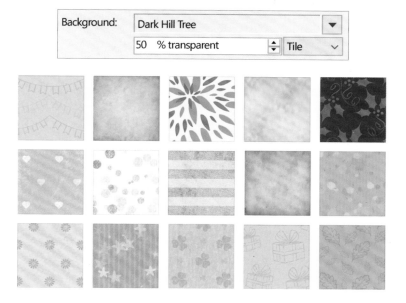

2.   Choose how the background will be displayed. To center the image on the page, choose **Center**. To stretch the image to fit the entire page, choose **Stretch**. To show a close-up of the image, choose **Zoom**. To show a series of the image, choose **Tile**.

3.   Choose the intensity of the image. At 0 percent, the image will look normal, while a higher percentage will fade the image so the report is easier to read.

Changing the Header or Footer

You can define a report's headers and footers (the lines of text at the top and bottom of the page).

1.   Access the report you want to change. In the editing toolbar, click the **Header/Footer** button.

2.   Change the header and footer options as necessary:

   •   **Show report title on every page.** Click this checkbox to display a header (the title) on each page of the report.

- **Show footer.** Click this checkbox to display a footer on each page of the report. Click **Include page number** to display a page number on the left side of the footer; click **Include print date** to display the current date on the right side of the footer; click **Include print time** to display the current time next to the current date.

3. Click **OK**.

Changing Fonts

You can change the appearance of the text in reports to make it more formal, more fun, or maybe just more readable.

1. Access the report you want to change. In the editing toolbar, click the **Fonts** Aa button.

2. In the Items to format list, click the text element, such as the report title, you want to change.

3. Choose a font from the **Font** drop-down list. You can also change the size of the font, its style, color, and alignment.

4. Click **OK** to save your changes.

Saving Reports

You can save a specific report in Family Tree Maker, or you can save a report in different file formats to export.

Saving the Settings for a Report

After you've customized a report, you can save your settings so you won't have to recreate these changes the next time you view the report. The settings you can save depend on the report, but generally include fact options, fonts, headers and footers, page layouts, and background images.

Note: You cannot save settings in one report and use them in another. For example, if you save settings in the Parentage Report, you cannot use these settings in the Kinship Report.

1. After you've modified the report, click the **Save settings** button in the editing toolbar.

2. A message asks if you want to use the current settings as the preferred settings for this report type. Click **Yes**.

Tip: To change back to the report's default settings, click the **Use report settings** button in the editing toolbar. Then choose **Default settings** and click **OK**.

Saving a Specific Report

If you like a report you've created, you'll probably want to save it. That way you can view it again without having to recreate it.

1. After you've modified a report, click the **Save report** button in the editing toolbar.

2. Enter a unique name for the report. For example, don't use generic terms like "Family Group Sheet" or "Custom Report".

3. Click **Save**.

Tip: To open a saved report, go to the Collection tab on the Publish workspace. In Publication Types, click **Saved Reports**. Then double-click the report you want to open.

Saving a Report as a File

You may want to save a report as a document or spreadsheet so you can share it easily with family or post it online.

1. Access the report you want to save.

2. Click the **Share** button above the editing panel. From the drop-down list, choose one of these options:

    - **Export to PDF.** An Adobe PDF (Portable Document Format) is useful because it keeps the formatting you select. If you print a report or send it to a relative, the report will look exactly as you see it on your monitor. You can't change a PDF within Family Tree Maker, and you need Adobe Reader to view it. (Reader can be downloaded for free from the Adobe website.)

    - **Export to CSV.** This spreadsheet format organizes information into fields (comma-separated values). Although you can export any report to a CSV file, it is most useful for statistical reports that use columns, such as the marriage report.

    - **Export to RTF.** This creates a basic text file but can include information such as text style, size, and color. This universal format can be read by nearly all text editing programs.

    - **Export to HTML.** Hypertext Markup Language is the standard language for creating and formatting Web pages.

    Each format has its own export options. After you choose a format type, you may be able to choose options such as text separators. Once you've made your selections, click **OK**.

3. Navigate to the location where you want to save the report. Then enter a name for it and click **Save**.

Printing a Report

1. Access the report you want to print.

2. Click the **Print** button above the editing panel.

3. When prompted choose a printer, select the number of copies, and choose a page range.

4. Click **Print**.

Sharing a Report

You can share reports with others—via email—in a variety of formats.

Note: You must be connected to the Internet and have a desktop email program to use this feature.

1. Access the report you want to email.

2. Click the **Share** button above the editing panel. From the drop-down list, choose one of these options:

    - **Send as PDF.** The Adobe PDF retains printer formatting and graphical elements so it resembles how the printed document will appear.

    - **Send as CSV.** This format organizes information into fields (comma-separated values) and is meant to be imported into spreadsheet programs.

    - **Send as RTF.** This creates a basic text file but can include information such as text style, size, and color. This universal format can be read by nearly all text editing programs.

    - **Send as Image.** This option lets you create an image of the report as a bitmap, JPEG, or other image format.

Each format has its own export options. After you choose a format type, you may be able to choose options such as page borders and text separators. Once you've made your selections, click **OK**. A file management window opens.

3. Navigate to the location where you want to save the report. Then enter a name for the report and click **Save**. Family Tree Maker opens a new email (with the file attached).

4. Send the email as you would any other.

Chapter Eleven
Creating a Family History Book

Wouldn't you love to have a printed family history to share your family stories, photographs, maps, and research? And what could be more convenient than using the same software to organize your family history *and* create a book to tell your ancestral story?

Family Tree Maker has a publishing tool to help you create a quality family history book that you and your family will enjoy for years to come. The tool is a desktop book-building feature built into the Family Tree Maker software. It's a great way to assemble a traditional genealogy using images, facts, charts, and reports from your tree.

The Desktop Book-Building Tool

Getting started with the book-building tool is easy because you can use the facts, charts, reports, and timelines already in your tree. Add some personal stories and photos and you've created a book you can email to family members or get printed at a copy shop.

Starting a Family History Book

1. Go to the **Collection** tab on the Publish workspace. In **Publication Types**, click **Books**.

2. Double-click **Genealogy Book**. The Save Book window opens.

3.   Enter a title for the book in the **Book name** field and click **Save**. The book opens in the text editor.

Importing a Book

If you created a book in Family Tree Maker 2006 or Version 16, you can import the book into your tree. However, because of differences between the old and new software, some items won't transfer, such as images, text formatting, and NGSQ reports.

Note: Before you import a book, make a backup of your tree. Also, you can only import books that have been created in Family Tree Maker.

1.   Choose **File>Import Books**.

2.   Navigate to the Family Tree Maker (.ftw) file that contains the book you want to import and click **Open**. A success message shows how many books and book items were imported.

3.   Click **OK**. The book is added to the Saved Books list.

4.   To view the imported book, go to the **Collection** tab on the Publish workspace. In **Publication Types**, click **Saved Books**.

5.   Double-click the book to open it in the text editor.

   If an item wasn't imported, you can click on the missing item in the outline to see an explanation of what has been left out— and in some cases, who the item was attached to.

This report or chart failed to import correctly or is not currently supported in this version of Family Tree Maker.

Type: BKI_FANDESCENDANT

Title: Descendant Fan Tree of Catherine Landis
Root Person: John Fitzgerald Kennedy

Accessing a Saved Book

1. Go to the **Collection** tab on the Publish workspace. In **Publication Types**, click **Saved Books**.

2. Double-click the book you want to open, or select its icon and then click the **Detail** tab. The book opens in the text editor.

Setting Up a Book

When you create a book you can enter the name of the author and title and add headers and footers.

1. Access the book you want to set up.

2. In the book panel toolbar, click the **Book Properties** button.

3. Change the book's properties as necessary:

    •   **Book title.** Enter the name of the book. This is the title that will appear in the book's headers and footers; it is not entered on the title page automatically.

    •   **Author.** Enter the author of the book.

    •   **Header.** Choose a header type from the drop-down list. Headers are typically the title of a book, but you can have no header, or a combination of the book title, chapter name, and page number. To change the header's font, click **Font** and choose a style and size from the drop-down list.

        Note: You can add or remove the header from a specific page using Item Properties. See "Changing an Item's Settings" on page 219.

- **Footer.** Choose a footer type from the drop-down list. Footers are typically page numbers, but you can have no footer, or a combination of the book title, chapter name, and page number. To change the footer's font, click **Font** and choose a style and size from the drop-down list.

  Note: You can add or remove the footer from a specific page using Item Properties. For instructions see "Changing an Item's Settings" on page 219.

- **Starting number.** Choose what page you want the body of the book to start on (the front matter—title page, table of contents, dedication, etc.—will be numbered separately).

- **Use Roman numerals.** Click this checkbox to use standard Roman numerals (i, ii, iii, iv) for the book's front matter— title page, table of contents, dedication, etc.

4. Click **OK**.

Adding Content to a Book

You can add any number of items to your family history book, including stories, photos, reports, charts, and even an automatically generated table of contents and index.

Adding Text

Don't let your family history book become a dry recitation of facts. Add interest by including family stories and memories. If your grandfather immigrated to America when he was young, don't just list this fact in an individual report. Include an excerpt from his journal that tells how he felt when he saw the Statue of Liberty.

Family Tree Maker has three options for entering text: you can manually type text, import text from a text file or document, or use Smart Stories to extract facts, sources, and notes in your tree (for more information on Smart Stories, see page 62).

Adding a Text Item

Before you can add stories, you'll need to add a text item to the book. A text item is basically a blank sheet of paper in the book text editor. Creating one is much like opening a new document in a word-processing program. You can use it for everything from an entire chapter to a simple page with a photo and a caption.

1.   Access the book you want to add a text item to. In the book panel toolbar, click the **Add Book Item** 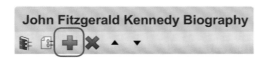 button.

The Add Book Item window opens.

2.   In **Publication type**, click **Other**. Then double-click **Smart Story (Text Item)**, or select its icon and then click **OK**. A blank page opens in the text editor.

Entering Text Manually

You can use the text editor to write your own family narratives.

1. Click a text item in the book outline.

2. Place the cursor where you want the text and begin typing.

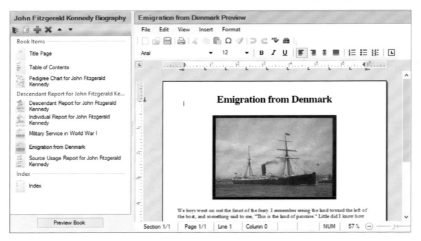

Importing Text from Another Document

If you've already written part of your book in another text editing program, you don't have to re-type your text or copy and paste sections into Family Tree Maker. You can import the entire .doc/.docx, .rtf/.rtfd, or .txt document at once—without losing formatting.

1. Create a new text item.

2. Select the text item in the book outline.

3. Place the cursor where you want the text. In the text editor, choose **File>Open**. A file management window opens.

4. Navigate to the document you want to import and click **Open**.

Formatting Text

The text formatting options available in Family Tree Maker are similar to most word-processing programs. You can change fonts, text size, alignment, tabs, and indents.

1. Click a text item in the book outline.

2. Format the text using these options:

   - **Change the font color, size, or style.** Select the text you want to change. Click **Format>Character**. The Font window opens. Make the necessary changes and click **OK**.

   - **Change the amount of space between lines of text.** Select a paragraph. Click **Format>Paragraph**. On the Formatting and Indents tab, choose a spacing option from the **Line spacing** drop-down list. Click **OK**.

   - **Change the indent of a paragraph.** Select a paragraph. Click **Format>Paragraph**. On the Formatting and Indents tab, choose new indents from the **Left** and **Right** drop-down lists. Click **OK**.

   - **Add a page break.** Place your cursor where you want the page break to occur. Click **Format>Paragraph**. On the Frame and Page Breaks tab, click the **Page break before** checkbox. Click **OK**.

   - **Change the document's tabs.** Click **Format>Tabs**. The Tabs window opens. Make the necessary changes and click **OK**.

Adding Images

What family history book would be complete without photos, letters, historical records, and maps? Family Tree Maker lets you add images from your family tree or images you've stored on your computer that you don't necessarily want to keep in your family tree—for example, clip art or embellishments.

1. Click a text item in the book outline.

2. Place your cursor where you want the image to appear.

3. Do one of the following:

    •   To use an image in your tree, choose **Insert>Image from Media Collection**. The Find Media Item window opens. Select the image and click **OK**.

    •   To use an image on your computer, choose **Insert>Image from File**. Navigate to the image you want and click **Open**.

Note: You can also add images linked to individuals by clicking the Media button on the Smart Story toolbar (for more information see page 67). Select the image you want and drag it to your document.

4. To align the image, use the alignment buttons on the toolbar. You can also move the image by dragging it to a new location.

5. To resize an image, click it. Then drag one of its square handles to change the size. To maintain the image's proportions, drag the image from one of its corners.

Adding a Chart or Report

You can add as many charts and reports to a book as you'd like. Make sure you choose ones that are appropriate for your audience. For example, you may want to share more personal and informal reports in a book meant for your children, but you'll want to remove facts about living relatives if you are sharing the book with other genealogists.

1. Access the book you want to add a chart or report to.

2. In the book panel toolbar, click the **Add Book Item** button.

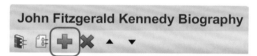

3. In the Add Book Item window, click the category for the chart or report you want to use. Then double-click the chart/report, or select its icon and click **OK**.

    Tip: You can also click **Saved Charts** or **Saved Reports** to use items you've already created.

4. Use the editing panel to customize the chart or report (for instructions see chapters 9 and 10).

Adding a Placeholder

If you want to incorporate a story, chart, or photo from outside Family Tree Maker, you can use a placeholder to reserve a specific number of pages until you're ready to add the information.

1. Access the book you want to add a placeholder to.

2. In the book panel toolbar, click the **Add Book Item** ✚ button.

3. In the Add Book Item window, click **Other**. Then double-click **Place Holder**, or select its icon then click **OK**.

4. Choose the number of pages you want to reserve from the **Number of pages** field.

    Tip: Give the placeholder a descriptive name so you don't forget what you were going to use it for. You can change its name by clicking the Book Item Properties button in the book panel toolbar.

Creating a Table of Contents

Family Tree Maker can generate a table of contents for a book automatically. If you make changes to a book (such as adding a chart or moving a chapter), the table of contents and its page numbers will be updated to reflect the changes.

Note: The table of contents is added after the title page. You can change the order of the front matter—table of contents, dedication, preface, etc.—but you cannot move the table of contents out of the front matter.

1. Access the book you want to add a table of contents to.

2. In the book panel toolbar, click the **Add Book Item** button.

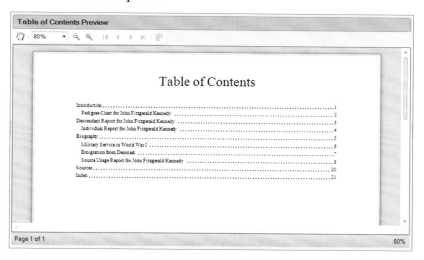

3. In the Add Book Item window, click **Other**. Then double-click **Table of Contents**, or select its icon and then click **OK**. The table of contents opens.

Although you cannot edit the table of contents, you can customize its font, size, and color by clicking the **Fonts** button under the "Table of Contents Options" heading.

Creating an Index of Individuals

Family Tree Maker can automatically generate a list of all individuals in the book's reports and charts (names mentioned in text items will *not* be included). If you make changes to the book (such as adding a new chart) Family Tree Maker will update the index to reflect the change.

Note: The index cannot be moved; it must be the last item in your book.

1.   Access the book you want to add an index to.

2.   In the book panel toolbar, click the **Add Book Item** button.

John Fitzgerald Kennedy Biography

3.   In the Add Book Item window opens, click **Other**. Then double-click **Index**, or select its icon then click **OK**. The index opens.

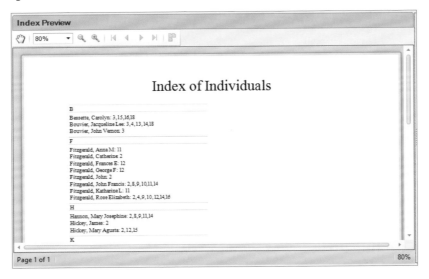

Although you cannot edit the index, you can customize its font, size, and color by clicking the **Fonts** button under the "Index Options" heading.

Organizing a Book

As your book grows, you may find that it has changed from the project you originally envisioned and that you need to make some adjustments. Perhaps you've uncovered additional records and photos and you want to rearrange a couple of chapters to include them. Family Tree Maker makes it easy to change titles, move chapters, or even delete sections you don't need.

Changing an Item's Settings

A Family Tree Maker book is made up of a variety of different book items: text items, charts, reports, etc. You can change settings for each book item.

1. Click an item in the book outline.

2. In the book panel toolbar, click the **Book Item Properties** button.

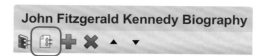

3. Change the item's settings using these options:

- **Change the item's title.** Enter a title in the **Item name** field. This is the title that will appear in the book's table of contents and this item's headers and footers.

- **Make this item start a new chapter.** Click the **This item begins a chapter** checkbox.

- **Make the first page of this item start on an odd-numbered (right-facing) page.** Click the **Start this item on an odd numbered page** checkbox. Typically each chapter starts on an odd-numbered page.

- **Prevent a page number from appearing on the first page of an item.** Click the **Do not print page number on the first page** checkbox. Typically chapter openers do not include a page number. You may also want to use this option for reports, charts, and full-page images.

- **Display headers in the item.** Click the **Include the header in this item** checkbox.

- **Display footers in the item.** Click the **Include the footer in this item** checkbox.

4. Click **OK**.

Rearranging Book Items

The book panel shows all the items in a book. The order in which they're displayed in this outline is the order in which they will be printed. You can change this order at any time.

1. Click the item you want to move in the book outline.

2. To change an item's order in the outline, select the item. Then click the **Move Up** ▲ and **Move Down** ▼ buttons in the book panel toolbar. (You can also drag items to the desired location.)

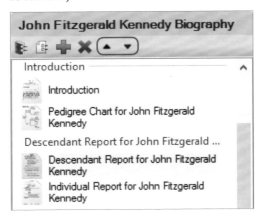

Deleting a Book Item

If you don't want a text item, report, or chart in your book, you can delete it.

1. Click the item you want to delete in the book outline.
2. Click the **Delete Book Item** button.
3. Click **Yes** to confirm.

Printing a Book at Home

When you're done creating a book, you can make copies on your home printer.

Tip: If you want to see what your book will look like when it is printed, click the **Preview Book** button below the book outline.

1. Access the book you want to print.
2. Click the **Print** button below the main toolbar.
3. When prompted choose a printer, select the number of copies, and choose a page range.
4. Click **Print**.

Exporting a Book

You can export your book as a PDF or text file and take it to a copy shop to be printed and professionally bound or email it to family members.

1. Access the book you want to export; then click the **Share** button below the main toolbar.
2. Choose **Export to PDF** or **Export to RTF** from the drop-down list. A file management window opens.
3. Navigate to the location where you want to save the book. Then enter a name for it and click **Save**.

Family Book Creator Plug-In

Family Book Creator by Stefan Harms is a plug-in for Family Tree Maker which turns your research into a detailed personalized book with just a few clicks.

Different book types and languages are supported. You may create your book documents directly in word processor file formats (DOCX, DOC, RTF, ODT) or platform independent file formats (PDF, EPUB, JPEG, PNG) without the need of having Microsoft Word or any other word processor or PDF application installed.

Family Book Creator is able to create the following types of books:

- Alphabetical family register
- Ancestors of the selected individual
- Descendants of the selected individual and preferred spouse
- Relatives of the selected individual

To get the plug-in, please visit www.familytreemaker.com and follow the **GIFT Collection** link.

Part Four
Managing Your Trees

Chapter Twelve
Working with Trees

In chapter 3 you learned how to create and import new trees. This chapter explains the many tools Family Tree Maker has to help you manage, share, and protect your trees.

Managing Your Trees

This section explains how to manage your trees effectively, whether you're working on one comprehensive tree or multiple trees.

Opening a Tree

When you launch Family Tree Maker, it automatically opens the last tree you were working in. You can switch to a different tree when necessary.

1.   On the main toolbar, click the tree drop-down list and choose the tree you want to open.

If the tree you want isn't in the drop-down list, click **Browse** to look for it on your hard drive. Navigate to the tree you want and click **Open**.

Note: If you try to open a GEDCOM, a tree file from a previous version of Family Tree Maker, or a file from another genealogy program, the software automatically opens the New Tree tab so you can import it (for instructions see "Importing a Tree" on page 25).

Viewing Information About a Tree

You can view a summary of your tree file, such as its size and the last day you created a backup. You can also see information about the people in your tree, for example, the number of marriages, individuals, and surnames.

1. Go to the **Current Tree** tab on the Plan workspace. A basic summary of your tree file appears at the top of the tab.

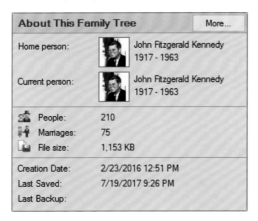

2. To see additional statistics, click the **More** button. The File Statistics window opens.

Renaming a Tree

You can change the name of a tree at any time.

1. On the main toolbar, click the tree drop-down list. Move the pointer over the tree, and then click **Rename Tree**.

2. Enter a new name for the tree and click **OK**.

   Note: Only the name of your FTM tree will change. The name of any linked Ancestry trees will not be changed.

Deleting a Tree

1. On the main toolbar, click the tree drop-down list. Move the pointer over the tree, and then click **Delete Tree**.

2. If you want to delete the media files that are linked to the tree, click **Move selected linked files** and select the files you'd like to delete. Then click **OK**.

Using Privacy Mode

If your tree contains personal information about living family members, you might want to "privatize" your tree before exporting a family history book or printing a family tree chart. In privacy mode information about living individuals, such as birth dates, will not be displayed. Be aware that you cannot edit the tree until you turn off privacy mode.

1. Click **File>Privatize File**. "Privatized" appears in the window's title bar and a checkmark appears next to the Privatize File option in the File menu.

2. To continue working in your tree, turn off privacy mode by clicking **File>Privatize File** again.

Exporting a Tree File

If you want to share your family tree with someone, you can export all or part of a tree as a GEDCOM—the standard file format used to transfer data between different genealogy software. (Be aware that only links to media files will be included in GEDCOMs.) You can also export your tree as a Family Tree Maker 2017 or a Family Tree Maker 2014.1 file.

TIP: To export a specific branch of your family tree, go to the People workspace. Select the person whose family you want to export. Right-click and choose **Export Branch**.

1. Click **File>Export**. If the information window appears, click **Continue**. The Export window opens.

2. Do one of the following:

    -   To export the entire tree, click **Entire file**.

    -   To export a saved Index list, click **Saved list**.

    -   To choose specific individuals to include in the file, click **Selected individuals**. The Filter Individuals window will open. Click a name and then click **Include** to add the person. When you're finished choosing individuals, click **Apply**.

3. Choose a GEDCOM or Family Tree Maker option from the **Output format** drop-down list.

4. To exclude information about living individuals, select the **Privatize living people** checkbox. Names and relationships will be exported, but facts and shared facts will not.

5. Choose the information you want to include in the export file:

    •   **Private facts.** Click this checkbox to export facts marked as private.

    •   **Private notes.** Click this checkbox to export notes marked as private.

    •   **Media files.** Click this checkbox to export all media files in your tree. Click the **Private media** checkbox to export media items marked as private.

    •   **Tasks.** Click this checkbox to export your research to-do list.

        Note: This option is not available for GEDCOMs.

    •   **Charts, reports, and books.** Click this checkbox to export charts, reports, and books you've saved.

        Note: This option is not available for GEDCOMs.

GEDCOM

Because your great-aunt may not use the same software you do, you'll need to share your family history with her in the GEDCOM format. GEDCOM stands for GEnealogical Data COMmunications; it allows genealogy files to be opened in any genealogy software program—on Macs or PCs.

- **Include only items linked to selected individuals.** Click this checkbox to export *only* tasks, notes, and media items that are linked to the individuals you're exporting.

6. Depending on the output format you have chosen, select the **Enable password protection** checkbox or the **Export as password-protected ZIP file** checkbox. The **Password** and **Confirm password** fields become available. Enter the password you want to use for protection of your exported tree. Make sure your password is not easy to guess. It should be at least eight characters long and contain digits as well as letters. You, or anyone you give the file to, will have to enter exactly the same password when opening or unpacking your exported tree. Passwords cannot be recovered, so it's a good idea to write the password down and keep it in a safe place.

7. Click **OK**.

8. If you are exporting to GEDCOM, choose the program into which the GEDCOM file is going to be imported.

9. Navigate to the location where you want to save the tree file.

   Note: Family Tree Maker automatically gives the exported file the same name as the original tree. If you want to use a different name, you can change it.

10. Click **Save**. A message tells you when your tree file has been exported successfully.

Backing Up Tree Files

Your family trees are important; not only do they contain your family's history, they represent hours of hard work. Unfortunately, computer files can be corrupted by viruses or accidentally deleted. You can preserve your family history through regular backups.

Then, if your original tree is damaged or you want to revert to a previous copy, you can restore it from the backup.

Tip: Family Tree Maker can back up a tree automatically every time you exit the program. To do this, click **Tools>Options** and make sure the **Automatically backup family file** checkbox is selected.

Backing Up a Tree File

1. Make sure the tree you want to back up is open and click **File>Backup**. The Backup window opens.

2. If you want a new name to distinguish your backup file from your original tree, enter a new name in the **Backup file name** field. For example, if you back up your trees to the same USB flash drive every time, and this backup file has the same name as the file that is already on the drive, then this backup will write over the original file.

3. Choose one of these backup types:

- **DVD or flash drive.** Click **Removable Media**. In the drop-down list, choose your DVD drive or flash drive.

- **Hard drive.** Click **Working directory** to save the backup to the folder where your current tree is saved; click **Custom directory** to choose a new location on your hard drive.

4. Choose the information you want to include in the backup:

    - **Media files.** Click this checkbox to include all media items from the tree's media folder.

    - **Historical events.** Click this checkbox to include historical events you've created or edited for timelines.

    - **Web favorites.** Click this checkbox to include your favorites list on the Web Search workspace.

5. If the tree is linked to an Ancestry tree, click **Allow restored file to resume syncing** so the backup file can be synced with the Ancestry tree if necessary.

6. Click **OK**. A message tells you when the tree file has been backed up successfully.

    Note: Backup files cannot be opened in other genealogy programs like GEDCOMs can. They can only be opened in the version of Family Tree Maker in which they were created.

Restoring a Tree from a Backup

If you need to use your backup file as your working tree, you can restore it when necessary.

1. Disable any anti-virus software running on your computer.

2. If your backup file has been copied to a DVD or other removable media, copy it back to your hard drive.

3. Click **File>Restore**. A file management window opens.

4. Navigate to the backup file you want to restore and click **Open**.

    Note: You can identify a backup file by its file extension (the letters after the file name). Family Tree Maker backups use .ftmb.

5. Enter a name for the restored tree file and click **Save**.

    The tree will open. Any info you entered in the original tree since you created this backup will not be included. Don't forget to reenable your anti-virus software.

Compressing a Tree File

As you work in a tree you will add and delete quite a bit of information. However, even when you delete info, the file size may not change. You should compress a tree periodically to remove unnecessary bits of data and optimize performance.

1. Click **Tools** > **Compact File**. The Compact File window opens.

2. To back up your tree file before you compress it, click the **Back up file before compacting** checkbox (recommended).

3. To have the tree file analyzed more deeply prior to compacting, select the **Perform extended analysis** option. This may significantly increase the duration of the compacting process.

4. Click **Compact**. If you chose to back up your file, the Backup window opens. Change any options as necessary and click **OK**.

5. When Family Tree Maker has finished compacting the tree file, a message appears showing how much the file size was reduced by. Click **OK**.

6. Repeat steps 1 through 5 until you get the result "reduced by 0.00%" or as close as you can get to it.

    Because file compression happens behind the scenes, you won't see changes in your tree, but you should notice better performance and a smaller overall tree file size.

Uploading a Tree to Ancestry

Chapter 3 explains how to start a new tree by downloading an existing tree from Ancestry. Family Tree Maker also lets you upload a tree to Ancestry. It's easy, free, and because your tree will be online, it can be shared with family around the world.

Note: To upload a tree to Ancestry, you do not need a subscription, but you must log in to your Ancestry account and have Internet access.

Uploading and Linking a Tree to Ancestry

When you upload a tree to Ancestry, you create a link between your desktop Family Tree Maker tree and its corresponding tree on Ancestry. This means that additions, deletions, or edits you make in your Family Tree Maker tree will be duplicated in your Ancestry tree (and vice versa). (For more information see "Working with Linked Trees" on page 238.)

Be aware that the time it takes to upload your tree is determined by tree size (including the size of the media collection) and the speed of your Internet connection. Your tree will be transmitted in the background in two stages. Media items are processed first and data is uploaded during the final stage. The tree will appear online when both media and tree data are uploaded.

Note: When you upload and link a tree to Ancestry, you must upload your entire tree; you can't choose which part of your tree is uploaded.

1. Open the tree you want to upload to Ancestry. Then go to the Plan workspace and click the **Current Tree** tab.

2. Click the **Upload and Link to Ancestry** button.

FamilySync - Access Via Ancestry

Not uploaded & linked

This tree is not linked or shared online

There are great benefits to having an online tree:
- It's free and easy to share with family and others
- You can access your tree from any Internet connection
- Changes you make to either tree appear in both places

Upload and Link to Ancestry...

3. Enter a name in the **New Ancestry Tree** field.

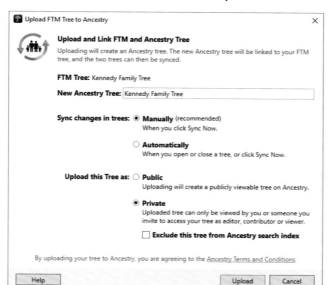

4. Choose whether you want to make your Ancestry tree public or private. See "Privacy Options for Ancestry Trees" below for more information.

Privacy Options for Ancestry Trees

When you upload your tree to Ancestry, you can choose between two levels of privacy:

- **Public.** If your tree is public, Ancestry subscribers can view your entire tree (except information about living individuals and private notes), and your tree will appear in search engines such as Google.
- **Private.** If your tree is private, limited information about individuals in your tree (name, birth year, birthplace) will still appear in Ancestry search results. No one will be able to view your entire tree or any attached photos and records unless he or she asks your permission and you grant it. You can also invite other people to view your tree.

5. If you don't want your private tree to appear in search results on Ancestry or third-party search engines such as Google, select the **Exclude this tree from Ancestry search index** checkbox.

6. Choose whether your Ancestry and FTM trees will be synced manually or automatically. (For more information on synchronization options, see "Setting Up Syncing" on page 239.)

7. Click **Upload**. A message lets you know when the tree has been uploaded successfully.

8. To view your tree on Ancestry, click the **View online tree now** checkbox and click **OK**.

Differences Between FTM and Ancestry Trees

Most content in your tree is uploaded and/or synced seamlessly between Family Tree Maker and Ancestry. However, because Ancestry and FTM trees are in different formats, there are a few differences you should be aware of.

Content	Differences
Facts	In general fact dates, places, and descriptions (including alternate facts) are the same in Family Tree Maker and Ancestry trees. However, some fact types have different labels. For example, the Physical Description fact in Family Tree Maker is the Description fact in Ancestry trees.
Media items	• The caption of a media item in Family Tree Maker is the same as the Picture name field on Ancestry. • Video items are not transferred between Family Tree Maker and Ancestry. • Media items attached to relationships in Family

Content	Differences
Media items (continued)	Tree Maker are uploaded to Ancestry as linked to each person individually, but not to the relationship. • Ancestry citation media you've merged into Family Tree Maker won't be re-uploaded to Ancestry. • Documents can't be uploaded to Ancestry trees in these formats: .exe, .dll, .bat, and .mht. • Photos that exceed 15MB will be resized when uploaded to Ancestry—your original file will not be affected. Images need to be in one of these formats: .jpeg, .bmp, .png, .gif, or .tif.
Notes	In Family Tree Maker you can create a variety of notes: person, research, fact, relationship, media, and source citation. Only person notes can be uploaded to Ancestry trees.
Places	Shortened display names and GPS coordinates in Family Tree Maker are not included in Ancestry trees.
Publications	Saved reports, charts, and books cannot be transferred from Family Tree Maker to Ancestry.
Privacy	In Family Tree Maker only you can view information you've entered for a living individual. In your Ancestry tree, only people you give permission to can view information about living individuals.
Web links	Web links are not uploaded, downloaded, or synced.
Sources	• Sources created with templates will transfer to Ancestry. Some fields cannot be uploaded online. • Media items attached to citations are uploaded; media items attached to sources are not.

Content	Differences
Stories	• A story created on Ancestry will become an .htm file in Family Tree Maker, which can be viewed in a Web browser. You can edit the text in a word-processing program. • Smart Stories created in Family Tree Maker will be text files (.rtf) in Ancestry. The story can't be viewed in your Ancestry tree but the document can be downloaded. (Smart Stories are uploaded only if they are attached to individuals.)

Working with Linked Trees

Family Tree Maker makes entering information into your tree fast and easy. It also contains powerful tools to help you organize your media items, cite sources, and create charts and reports. But because the program is on your desktop, sharing your tree with others can be time-consuming, and, if you don't have a laptop, you won't have access to your tree on the go.

Fortunately FamilySync gives you the freedom to view and update your tree no matter where you are. First, create your tree in Family Tree Maker. Then upload and link it to Ancestry. When you go to the library or a family member's home—anywhere with Internet access—make changes to your Ancestry tree online. Then sync the changes to your FTM tree when you get home. (You can also download and link a tree you've already created on Ancestry. For information see "Downloading a Tree from Ancestry" on page 26.)

Each Ancestry tree can link to multiple FTM trees. It's not necessary to break an old link to download a tree to a new computer. To link the trees on multiple computers to a single Ancestry tree, follow these steps:

1. Back up your FTM tree manually, including media and sync information. (See "Backing up a Tree File", page 231).

2. Copy the backup file to the other computer with a flash drive.

3. On the other computer, restore your tree from the backup.

The changes made in any of the trees can be applied to other trees automatically or manually. The core data in your linked trees is synchronized in all directions. But some types of data will not sync, remaining only on the computer they were created on.

> Note: For more information on what does and doesn't sync, open Family Tree Maker Help from the **Help** menu and search for the "Syncing Local and Online Trees" topic.

Setting Up Syncing

When you link your FTM and Ancestry trees together, you can choose how your trees will be synchronized. You have two options:

-   **Manually.** You can synchronize your trees by clicking the **Sync Now** button on the **Current Tree** tab or clicking the Ancestry Sync icon and choosing "Sync Now" from the drop-down.

-   **Automatically.** Family Tree Maker checks for changes when you open a tree or close the program. If it detects differences between the trees, it synchronizes the changes automatically. You can also sync your trees any time by clicking the **Sync Now** button on the **Current Tree** tab.

You can also choose whether or not Family Tree Maker will display a list of changes you've made to your Ancestry and FTM trees that you can review before syncing.

Changing Your Current Sync Setting

When you upload or download a linked tree, you will choose how your trees will be synced. You can change this setting at any time.

1. Go to the **Current Tree** tab on the Plan workspace.

2. Click the **Sync Now** button and choose "Sync Options" from the drop-down. The Sync Options window opens.

3. Click **Automatically** or **Manually**.

4. To download images of historical records from Ancestry when your trees sync, select the **Download Ancestry Citation Media** checkbox.

5. Click **OK**.

Creating a Log of Recent Sync Changes

You can set up FamilySync so that every time you sync your Ancestry and FTM trees you can view a list of recent changes—the number of people, sources, and media items that have been added, updated, or deleted from your tree since the last sync.

1. Go to the **Current Tree** tab on the Plan workspace.

2. Click the **Sync Now** button and choose "Sync Options" from the drop-down. The Sync Options window opens.

3. Select the **Show Change Log before finalizing sync** checkbox.

4. Select the **Proceed with sync after 60 seconds** checkbox to have Family Tree Maker automatically close the Sync Change Log window and complete the sync.

5. Click **OK**. The next time your trees are synced, you'll see the Sync Change Log (fig. 12-1).

Figure 12-1. The Sync Change Log.

The number of items deleted from the trees, if there are any, is displayed in red. You will be asked to confirm deletion if you proceed.

To proceed with the sync, click the **Continue** button. To reject the changes, click the **Cancel Sync** button. Click the **View/Print Details** button to see specific details about what changes will be included in the sync.

Viewing a Tree's Sync Status

The Ancestry Sync icon in the upper-right corner lets you see at a glance whether your FTM and Ancestry tree are synced. A check mark icon means that the trees are up-to-date; an icon with two vertical arrows means that you have changes waiting to be synced (fig. 12-2).

Figure 12-2. Left, trees are in sync; right, trees need to be synced.

The Ancestry Sync icon also displays the sync weather report status. See "Getting Sync Weather Reports" on page 243.

You can also see the date and time when your tree was last synced on the Current Tree tab on the Plan workspace (fig. 12-3).

Figure 12-3. Date and time of last sync.

Syncing Trees Manually

You can sync your tree manually at any time. However, be aware that you can't work in your Ancestry or FTM tree until synchronization is complete.

On the Plan workspace, click the **Current Tree** tab; then click the **Sync Now** button. On other workspaces, click the Ancestry Sync icon and choose "Sync Now" from the drop-down.

> Note: You can't sync your trees from Ancestry; you must use Family Tree Maker. To see the changes in your Ancestry tree, you'll need to reload or refresh the Ancestry website in your Web browser.

Getting Sync Weather Reports

Wouldn't it be great if you could know when there was a problem with syncing so you could just stay away for a time and come back when it was safe? That was the simple idea behind the Sync Weather Report we've built into Family Tree Maker 2017. Now each time you go to sync, if there's a reason you should maybe think twice, a window pops up to say so. The red window appears if the sync system is down, or if syncing is for some reason downright dangerous. This status is actually a kind of "kill switch" and syncing is temporarily disabled. The orange window appears when caution is in order. You can still sync but the Weather Report message system lets us tell you what's up.

In fact, you don't even have to try syncing a tree to find out what the sync weather is like. Just take a look at the Ancestry Sync icon, which can be found in the top-right corner of the application window and in the FamilySync panel in the bottom-left part of the Current Tree tab on the Plan workspace. It not only displays the sync status, it lets you instantly see the latest weather report as well:

 No problems found, safe to sync.

 Problems may occur, syncing is not recommended.

 Serious connection problems, syncing is impossible.

Resolving Conflicts Between Linked Trees

When you change the same fact in your FTM and Ancestry trees, you'll need to choose which information to keep (fig. 12-4). For example, if you change a deathplace in Family Tree Maker and a family member changes the same deathplace in your Ancestry tree, when you try to sync your trees, you'll be prompted to fix the issue.

1. Do one of the following:

    •   To keep the information entered in Family Tree Maker, click **Overwrite conflicts with Family Tree Maker data**.

    •   To keep the information entered in the Ancestry tree, click **Overwrite conflicts with Ancestry data**.

    •   To manually choose which information to keep, click **Resolve conflicts manually**.

Figure 12-4. A message showing conflicts between linked trees.

2. Click **Continue**. If you are overwriting data, the sync continues. If you are resolving the conflict manually, choose the facts you want to keep and click **Continue** again.

    Important: Deletions always take priority over other changes. For example, if you delete an individual in your Ancestry tree and update the same individual's birthplace in your FTM tree, when you sync the trees together the individual will be deleted.

Unlinking Trees

If you no longer want your FTM and Ancestry trees linked together, you can remove the connection between them.

Warning: If you unlink your FTM and Ancestry trees, changes will no longer be synchronized, and you cannot relink the trees, but you can upload or download the tree again to create a new link. Also note that Ancestry hints will not appear in an unlinked tree.

1. Click the Ancestry Sync icon in the top-right corner of any workspace and choose **Unlink Tree** from the drop-down list.

2. Click **Unlink**.

Changing Privacy Settings

When you upload a tree to Ancestry, you choose whether your Ancestry tree will be public (the default) or private. However, you can change its privacy settings at any time. (For more information on the differences between public and private trees, see page 235.)

1. Go to the **Current Tree** tab on the Plan workspace.

2. Click the **Sync Now** button and choose "Manage Online Tree Privacy" from the drop-down. The Tree Settings page opens.

3. Click **Public Tree** to let other Ancestry subscribers view your

tree; click **Private Tree** to prevent others from viewing your tree.

Note: If your tree is private, Ancestry subscribers can still see names, birth dates, and birthplaces from your tree in search results. However, to see your full tree or any attached photos and records, they'll have to ask you for permission. If you don't want your tree to appear in search results either, select the **Also prevent your tree from being found in searches** checkbox.

4. Click **Save Changes**.

Inviting Others to View Your Ancestry Tree

You can invite friends and family to view your Ancestry tree. You can even let them add new information or photos.

Warning: Anyone assigned the role of "editor" can add, edit, or delete information in your Ancestry tree. These changes will be made to your FTM tree when the trees are synced together.

1. Go to the **Current Tree** tab on the Plan workspace.

2. Click the **Invite to Online Tree** button. The Tree Settings window opens.

    Note: If you've already invited people to your tree, you'll need to click the **Sync Now** button and choose "Manage Online Tree Invitees" to invite more people to your tree.

3.   Click the **Invite people** button.

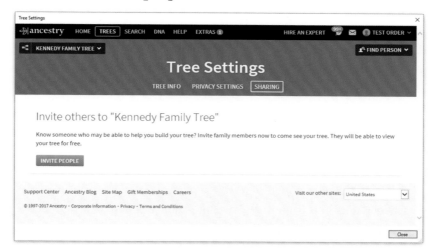

4.   Enter the person's email or Ancestry username to address the invitation and assign the person one of these roles: editor, contributor, guest.

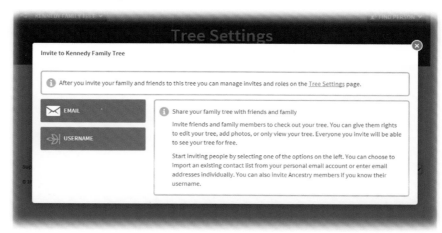

5.   If you want, include a personal message to the invitee. Then click **Send Invites**.

Roles in Ancestry Trees

When you invite people to view your tree, they can participate in different ways, depending on the role you assign them:

- **Editor.** Editors can add, edit, or delete anyone in your tree, add stories and photos, and leave comments. They can also see living individuals. Editors cannot delete or rename the tree, change tree settings, or invite others to the tree.
- **Contributor.** Contributors can add photos or stories to your tree, but they cannot add or edit people. You can choose whether or not they see living individuals.
- **Guest.** Guests can only view your tree and leave comments. You can choose whether or not they see living individuals.

Chapter Thirteen
Tools and Preferences

Using Family Tree Maker Tools

If you need some extra help calculating approximate birth dates, understanding how individuals are related to each other, or creating a to-do List, Family Tree Maker has several tools that can help.

Soundex Calculator

Soundex is a term familiar to serious family historians. It's a coding system used by the government to create indexes of U.S. census records (and passenger lists) based on how a surname sounds rather than how it is spelled. This was done to compensate for potential spelling and transcription errors. For example, "Smith" may be spelled "Smythe," "Smithe," or "Smyth." Using Soundex, these "Smiths" are all identified by the same code (S530). You can use Soundex to find surnames that use the same code and then search for ancestors using all these surname variations.

Click **Tools>Soundex Calculator**. Then enter a surname in the Name field, or click Index to select someone in your tree.

Soundex Calculator   ✕

Name   Kennedy   ▤ Index

Soundex value: K530

                               Close   Help

Relationship Calculator

The relationship calculator helps you identify how two people in your tree are related, shows an individual's nearest common relative, and gives his or her canon and civil numbers.

Note: Canon and civil numbers indicate the degree of relationship between individuals. Canon laws (used in the United States) measure the number of steps back to a common ancestor. Civil degree measures the total number of steps from one family member to another.

1.   Click **Tools>Relationship Calculator**. In the first field, you'll see the home person. In the second field, you'll see the individual who is the current focus of the tree.

2.   To change the individuals whose relationship you're calculating, click the **Person from people index** button next to a name (the button with an index card). In the Index of Individuals window, select a new person and click **OK**.

The individuals' relationship is listed underneath their names. If they have multiple connections (for example, if they are cousins who married), click the drop-down list to see each relationship. You can also see how the individuals are related in the Path section.

Date Calculator

You can use the date calculator to figure out an individual's birth year, age at the time of a specific event, or the date of an event. For example, if you know the date your grandmother was married and you know how old she was when she got married, you can determine the approximate year she was born.

1.   Click **Tools>Date Calculator**. The date calculator opens.

2. Use this chart to help you enter dates into the calculator:

To calculate this	Do this
A birth date	• Click **Birth date**. • Enter a date in the **Date of known event** field. • Enter the individual's age in the **Age at time of event** fields.
The date of a specific event	• Click **Other event date**. • Enter a date in the **Known birth date** field. • Enter the individual's age in the **Age at time of event** fields.
An individual's age on a specific date	• Click **Age**. • Enter a date in the **Known birth date** field. • Enter a date in the **Date of known event** field.

3. Click **Calculate**. The calculated event date or age appears.

Name Converter

If you import another person's genealogy file into your tree, you may find that each file has recorded names differently; your surnames may be in all caps while theirs may not. You can use the convert names tool to format all names in your tree at once.

1. Click **Tools>Convert Names**. The Convert Names window opens.

2. To capitalize the first letter in each name, click **First Middle Surname**. To capitalize the first letter of the first and middle names and capitalize the entire surname, click **First Middle SURNAME**.

3. Click **OK**.

Find Individual Tool

You can use any fact in your tree (such as occupation or burial) to locate either a specific individual or a group of individuals who fit specific criteria. For example, you can search for everyone in your tree who lived in Illinois at the time of the 1850 census. Or, you can find out which individuals are buried in the same cemetery.

Note: The Find Individual tool searches Place and Description fields; Date fields cannot be searched.

1. Click **Edit>Find Individual**. The Find Individual window opens.

2. Choose the type of fact you want to search from the drop-down list. Then enter your search term and click **Find**.

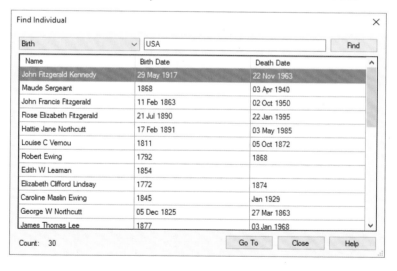

3. If you want to view a specific individual, click his or her name in the search results and click **Go To**.

Automatic Reference Numbers

Some family historians use reference numbers to identify people in their trees, particularly if the tree contains individuals with identical names. Family Tree Maker can assign reference numbers to individuals (Person ID), relationships (Relationship ID), or both.

Note: If you have entered your own reference numbers, Family Tree Maker will not overwrite them.

1. Click **Tools>Options**. Then click the **References** tab.

2. Click **Use individual reference numbers** to choose how numbers are assigned to individuals; click **Use relationship reference numbers** to choose how numbers are assigned to relationships.

3. Click **Numbers only** to assign numbers, starting with 1. Click **Prefix** to add a prefix before the number (you can enter numbers, letters, and/or symbols). Click **Numbers plus suffix** to add a suffix after the number (you can enter numbers, letters, and/or symbols).

4. Click **OK**.

Global Birth Order Tool

In the family group view, you can change the order in which children are displayed in a family by clicking the Move up and Move down buttons. If you always want to display children in your tree by birth order, you can use this tool to change them all at once.

1. Click **Tools>Sort All Children by Birth**.
2. If you want to back up your tree file before you sort children, click the **Back up file before sorting** checkbox (recommended).
3. Click **Sort**.

Research To-Do List

Whether you are a new user or an experienced family historian, the to-do list can help you keep track of the research you've already done and create tasks for your next steps. You can add research tasks for specific individuals or general tasks for your entire tree; tasks can be as simple as sending an email to a cousin or as complicated as locating an entire family in the 1940 census.

Creating a To-Do Task

When you create a task, you can choose the priority of the task, the category it fits in, and its due date.

Note: This section explains how to add tasks for specific individuals. You can also add tasks to the tree's to-do list on the Current Tree tab on the Plan workspace.

1. Go to the **Person** tab for a specific individual (on the People workspace). Click the **Tasks** tab.

2.   Click the **New** button in the Tasks toolbar. The Add Task window opens.

3.   Enter the task in the **Description** field. For example, "Look for Madeline's birth information in Highland, Utah."

4.   Click **Edit** to choose a category for the task. Choose a category or create a category and click **OK**. (For more information see "Creating Task Categories" below.)

5.   Choose a deadline for the task from the **Due date** drop-down list. Then choose a priority. (Assign a high priority to the tasks you want to accomplish first.) When you're finished click **OK**.

Tip: You can print the to-do list for this individual by clicking the Print button on the Tasks toolbar. To print a list of all tasks in your tree, use the Task List report on the Publish workspace.

Creating Task Categories

Each task you create can be assigned to a category. You can add categories that are useful to your research.

1. Go to the **Current Tree** tab on the Plan workspace. In the Tasks section, you can see your current to-do list.

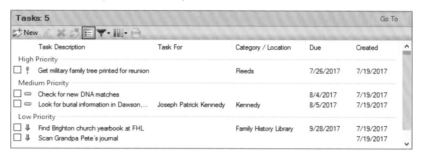

2. Click **New**. The Add Task window opens. Click **Edit**. The Category/Location window opens, showing all available categories.

3. Click **Add**. The Add Category Name window opens.

4. Enter a name in the **Category name** field and click **OK**. Click **OK** again.

Marking a Task as Complete

When you finish a task on your to-do list, you'll want to mark it as complete. Go to the **Current Tree** tab on the Plan workspace. In the Tasks section, click the checkbox next to the task.

Tip: To delete a task, click its name; then click the red (X) button in the Tasks toolbar.

Sorting the To-Do List

You can filter the to-do list in various ways. For example, you can sort the list to show which tasks are done or still pending.

1.   Go to the **Current Tree** tab on the Plan workspace.

2.   Click the **Filter tasks** button and choose one of these options from the drop-down list:

     •   To show every task you've entered, choose **Show All Tasks**.

     •   To show unfinished tasks, choose **Show Uncompleted Tasks**.

     •   To show tasks that belong to a specific category, choose **Filter by Task Categories**.

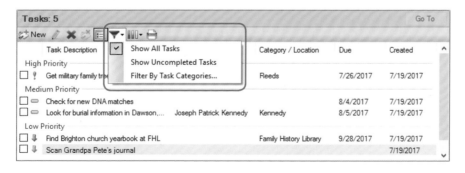

Tip: You can change what information is displayed for each task. Click the **Show/Hide columns** button in the Tasks toolbar. Then, from the drop-down list, select or deselect specific columns.

Setting Up Preferences

Family Tree Maker is a powerful program with many features and options. To get the most out of the software, you might want to take a minute and define a few key preferences.

General Preferences

You can set some preferences that affect the interface and general workings of Family Tree Maker.

1.   Click **Tools>Options**. Then click the **General** tab.

2.   Change these preferences as necessary:

- **Default directory for new tree files.** To change the default location where trees are saved on your hard drive, click **Browse** and choose a new folder.

- **Automatically check for program updates when connected to the Internet.** Click this checkbox if you want Family Tree Maker to look for software updates when you're online. You'll be alerted if an update exists.

- **Show LDS information.** Click this checkbox if you want to display LDS fields such as sealings and baptisms.

- **Use large fonts.** Click this checkbox to make fonts in the software larger and more readable.

Note: A larger font may help readability, but some labels may not display correctly or be cropped.

- **Use caption instead of filename for media display.** Click this checkbox to sort media items by the captions you've given them; otherwise media items will be sorted and displayed by file name.

- **Automatically backup family file.** Click this checkbox to create backups of your trees automatically when you close the program. If your original tree is ever lost or damaged, you can use the backup to restore your information.

- **Crop portrait displays.** Click this checkbox to resize portrait images so that they fill the frame.

  Note: The actual images in your tree will not be modified. Also, you cannot choose to resize individual thumbnails. This option resizes every portrait in your tree.

- **Show Sync Weather status on Ancestry Sync icon.** Click this checkbox to display the sync weather status badge on the Ancestry Sync icon.

- **Color theme.** Choose the color theme you want from the drop-down list: default for Ancestry is light green; Windows is classic blue; or you can select your current Windows display.

- **PDF driver.** If you don't want to use the default PDF driver, you can choose your own from the list.

- **Merging Default.** Choose a default method of dealing with differences when merging trees.

Online Searching Preferences

You can determine whether or not Family Tree Maker will search Ancestry and FamilySearch for matching records and trees when you're connected to the Internet.

1. Click **Tools>Options**. Then click the **General** tab.

2. Change these preferences as necessary:

    - **Show hints from Ancestry.** Select this checkbox to have
      Family Tree Maker search Ancestry for individuals in your
      tree when an Internet connection is available.

      You'll see a green leaf (or hint) next to an individual when
      possible matches have been found. If you deselect this op-
      tion, you can still search Ancestry for your family members
      on the Web Search workspace.

    - **Exclude Ancestry tree hints.** Select this checkbox to ex-
      clude hints from family trees submitted by other Ancestry
      users.

    - **Show hints from FamilySearch.** Select this checkbox to have
      Family Tree Maker search FamilySearch.org for individuals
      in your tree when an Internet connection is available.

      You'll see a blue square (or hint) next to an individual when
      possible matches have been found. If you deselect this option,
      you can still search FamilySearch for your family members
      on the Web Search workspace.

    - **Show Web Search introduction screen.** Select this checkbox
      to display Web Search help when you begin an online search.

Fastfields Preferences

Fastfields speed up data entry by automatically filling in repetitive
data as you type. For example, if you type "San Jose, California,
USA" into a place field then go to another place field and begin to
type "San," Family Tree Maker will recognize the similarity and

suggest "San Jose, California, USA." By default, all Fastfields are used, but you can turn off any you wish.

1. Click **Tools>Options**. Then click the **General** tab.

2. In the **Use fastfields for** section, click the checkbox for each type of field you want to turn off Fastfields for: names, places, sources, and/or fact descriptions.

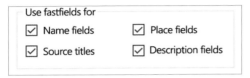

Spell Checking Preferences

You can choose which terms the spell check should ignore. By default these include words in uppercase and HTML tags.

Tip: You can use the dictionary to add unusual family surnames or locations that you want the spell checker to ignore.

1. Click **Tools>Options**. Then click the **General** tab.

2. Click the **Spell Check Options** button.

Fastfields

Fastfields save you time by automatically filling in some types of information. Perhaps you noticed as you typed an individual's name that the last name was completed for you. This is because name fields, among others, are Fastfields.

Location Fastfields remember the places you've entered in a tree. As you type a location, Family Tree Maker suggests possible matches. Use the keyboard arrows, mouse, or trackpad to highlight the correct location and press Enter to select it. You can also keep typing a name to override the Fastfields suggestion.

Fact Display Preferences

The person editing panel on the Person tab includes a Sources tab. If you want, you can also display media and notes tabs.

1. Click **Tools>Options**. Then click the **General** tab.

2. In the **Fact display** section, click the checkbox for each type of tab you want to display on the person editing panel.

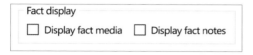

Date Preferences

Family Tree Maker lets you change how dates are formatted.

1. Click **Tools>Options**. Then click the **Names/Dates/Places** tab.

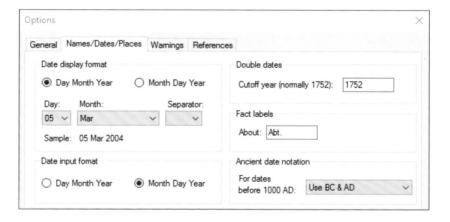

2. Change these date preferences as necessary:

    •   **Date display format.** Choose how dates are displayed. Click **Day Month Year** to show the day before the month (07 January 2017). By default, Family Tree Maker displays dates in this accepted genealogical date standard. Click **Month Day Year** to show the month before the day (January 7, 2017).

Click the drop-down lists to choose different formats for the day, month, and date separator.

- **Date input format.** Choose how Family Tree Maker interprets dates you enter: day, month, year, or month, day, year. For example, if you enter "6/7/2014" Family Tree Maker can read this as June 7th or July 6th.

- **Double dates.** Change the year in this field to change the default double date cutoff year. If you do not want double dates to print, set the double date cutoff year to zero.

  Note: Calendars in Europe and the United States changed in 1752—moving from Julian to Gregorian. In the Julian system, the first day of the year was 25 March. In today's Gregorian system, 1 January is the first day of the year. Dates that fall between January and March of 1752 can be interpreted in two ways, and some genealogists prefer to show both dates. For example, February 22 could fall in the year 1750 according to the Gregorian calendar, so the date would be noted as 22 February 1750/51.

- **Fact labels.** To display a different abbreviation for the term "About" (meaning "circa"), enter your preferred label.

- **Ancient date notation.** Choose whether dates before 1000 AD are displayed with BC/AD or BCE/CE.

Name Preferences

Family Tree Maker lets you determine how names are displayed in the Index on the People workspace. You can include titles, alternate names, and married names for females.

1.   Click **Tools>Options**. Then click the **Names/Dates/Places** tab.

2. Change these preferences as necessary:

- **Use AKA if available after middle name.** Click this checkbox to have Also Known As names included with the preferred name (for example, Bobbitt, Mary Eliza "Mollie").

- **Use AKA if available as an additional entry.** Click this checkbox to give Also Known As names their own entries in the Index (for example, Hannah Willis and Anna Willis).

- **Use titles if available.** Click this checkbox to have titles included with the preferred name (for example, Hoyt, Captain Samuel).

- **Use married names for females.** Click this checkbox to list women by their married (and maiden) names (for example, Hoyt, Maria Hitchcock).

Place Preferences

Family Tree Maker lets you determine whether place names entered in your tree are compared against the software's location database.

1. Click **Tools>Options**. Then click the **Names/Dates/Places** tab.

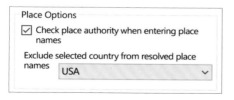

2. Change these preferences as necessary:

- **Check place authority when entering place names.** Click this checkbox to have Family Tree Maker compare each place you enter against its database of locations. This keeps your locations in standard formats and consistent throughout your tree.

- **Exclude selected country from resolved place names.** When you enter a place name, you usually include a country. However, if most events occur in the same country (for example, if most of your ancestors were born and died in England), you may not want to include that country's name in place fields and charts and reports. To keep a country's name from appearing, choose it from the drop-down list.

Warning and Alert Preferences

Family Tree Maker can automatically check your tree for problems and alert you if it detects a possible error, such as unusual dates.

1. Click **Tools>Options**. Then click the **Warnings** tab.

2. The **Show warnings for non-critical errors** section lets you choose how you want Family Tree Maker to handle minor errors. Change these preferences as necessary:

- **Show alerts for unlikely birth, death, and marriage dates.** Click this checkbox to get alerts when you enter dates that don't seem accurate (for example, a death date that occurs earlier than a birth date).

- **Show unrecognized place name indicators.** Click this checkbox to get alerts when Family Tree Maker doesn't recognize a location you've entered.

    Note: This option is not available if you deselected the "Check place authority" option on the Names/Dates/Places tab.

- **Show informational alerts.** Click this checkbox to get alerts when you update your tree—for example, when you change the home person or edit an individual's name.

- **Show prompt when sorting children in the family view.** Click this checkbox to get alerts when you manually sort children in the family group view.

- **Show backup reminder before critical operations.** Click this checkbox to be reminded to back up your tree before completing tasks like merging duplicate individuals.

- **Double dates.** If Family Tree Maker detects double dates, you can leave the dates as they are, use formatting to show both dates, or be prompted for instructions.

- **Titles in name fact.** If Family Tree Maker detects a title such as Reverend, Captain, or Sir in a Name fact, you can leave the title in the Name fact, move the title to the Title fact, or be prompted for instructions.

- **One- or two-digit years.** If Family Tree Maker detects years entered with one or two digits, you can accept the date as it is, change the date to the most recent century, or be prompted for instructions.

- **Text in quotes.** If Family Tree Maker detects nicknames (indicated by quotes) in a Name fact, you can leave the nickname in the Name fact, move the nickname to the AKA fact, or be prompted for instructions.

- **Copy media files.** When you add a media file to your tree, you can choose whether or not to automatically copy the file to the Family Tree Maker media folder or be prompted for instructions.

- **Auto-populate Smart Stories.** When you create a Smart Story, you can start with a blank page, a page populated with information about the individual and his or her family, or be prompted for instructions.

Managing Facts

Facts are the essential building blocks of your tree, where you record the details about your family. In order to capture the information you care about, you might want to create your own facts or change which fields appear in predefined facts.

Creating a Custom Fact

You can create custom facts that work for your family tree. For example, if you are tracking your ancestors by census records, you can make a custom fact for each census year.

1.   Click **Edit>Manage Facts**. The Manage Facts window opens.

2.   Click **New**. The Add Custom Fact window opens.

3.   Change the fact as necessary:

- **Fact label.** Enter the name of the fact as it will appear on the Person tab.

- **Short label.** Enter a short name (up to six characters) for the fact that will appear on the Tree tab editing panel.

- **Abbreviation.** Enter an abbreviation (up to three characters) for the fact that will appear in reports.

- **Fact type.** Choose **Individual fact** if the fact applies to one person, such as birth or death. Choose **Shared fact** if the fact applies to more than one individual, such as marriage.

- **Fact options.** Choose the fields that you want to appear for the fact: Date and Place; Date, Place, and Description; or Description only.

- **Private by default.** Click this checkbox to make this fact type private. You can change privacy for a specific fact on the Person tab.

- **Fact sentence.** To change the default sentence, see "Modifying a Fact Sentence" on page 271.

4. Click **OK**.

Modifying a Predefined Fact

While you can't rename or delete predefined facts, you can choose which fields are included as part of the fact. For example, you can modify the Cause of Death fact so that only the Description field is included.

1. Click **Edit>Manage Facts**. The Manage Facts window opens.

2. Click the predefined fact that you want to modify. Then click **Properties**. The Fact Properties window opens.

3. In **Fact options**, choose the fields you want for the fact.

4. Click the **Private by default** checkbox to make this fact type private. You can change privacy for a specific fact on the Person tab.

5. Click **OK**.

Modifying a Fact Sentence

When you create an Ahnentafel, descendant report, or Smart Story, Family Tree Maker generates descriptive sentences for each fact or event. You can change the wording and choose what info is included. For example, the default burial sentence looks like this: Robert Gedge was buried on 1 Sept 1888 in Attleborough, England. If you record cemetery names, you could add this to the sentence: Robert Gedge was buried in the All Saint's Cemetery in Attleborough, England, on 1 Sept 1888.

1. Click **Edit>Manage Facts**. The Manage Facts window opens.

2. Click **New** or select the fact you want to modify and click **Properties**. The Fact Properties window opens. The Fact sentence field displays the current sentence—a combination of text and predefined data variables.

3. To change the text, simply add, delete, or type over it. To change which variables are in the sentence, delete the variable or choose a new one from the **Insert Fact Data** drop-down.

    Tip: If you don't like your changes and want to use the default sentence, click **Insert Fact Data** and choose **Reset Fact Sentence**.

    The Example field shows what the fact sentence will look like. For example, if you deselect the Description checkbox, you can see what the sentence will be if the Description field for the fact is blank.

Managing Historical Events

An individual's timeline and the Timeline report can include historical events. You can edit or delete any historical event. You can also add entries that are relevant to your family history, such as international events that caused your ancestors to emigrate.

1. Click **Edit>Manage Historical Events**. The Manage Historical Events window opens.

2. To delete an event, click the entry; then click **Delete**.

3. To add an event, click the **New** button. The Add/Edit Historical Event window opens.

4. Change the historical event as necessary:

    •   **Event title.** Enter a short title for the event.

    •   **Event date.** Enter the date or date range of the event.

    •   **Place where event occurred.** Enter the location of the event.

- **Category.** Choose a historical category from the drop-down list or add your own categories. You can also edit and delete the default categories.

- **Description.** Enter a summary of the historical event.

5.   Click **OK**.

Customizing the Tree Tab Editing Panel

By default, these facts appear on the editing panel of the Tree tab in the People workspace: name, sex, birth date and place, death date and place, marriage date and place. If you often record burials or christenings, you can add these facts to the editing panel so you can enter the information more easily.

1.   Go to the **Tree** tab on the People workspace. The editing panel appears with its default facts.

2. Click **Customize View**. The Customize View window opens.

3. In the Individual facts section or the Shared facts section, click
    the fact you'd like to add to the editing panel; then click the
    right arrow button to add the fact to the Selected facts sections.

4. To change the order in which facts display on the panel, click
    a fact in the Selected facts section and click the up and down
    arrows.

5. Click **OK**. The editing panel now includes the new facts.

Entering User Information

You can enter information that identifies you as the creator of
a tree. This info is automatically added to your tree file if you
export and send it to another family member or researcher.

1. Click **Tools>User Information**. The User Information window
    opens.

2. Enter your information and click **OK**.

Chapter Fourteen
Family Tree Problem Solver

No matter how organized you are or how carefully you enter information, errors can creep into your tree. Whether you've added a child to the wrong family or spelled your ancestor's name incorrectly, Family Tree Maker makes it easy to clean up your tree.

Straightening Out Relationships

At some point in your research you may discover that a certain individual doesn't belong in your tree and you need to delete him or her. Or maybe you added a child to the wrong family. Cleaning up relationship issues as soon as you find them keeps them from multiplying.

Merging Duplicate Individuals

After months and years of gathering names and dates, your family tree may become a bit disorderly. You might discover that Flossie and Florence are actually the same person. If you've entered duplicate individuals, you should merge them together (instead of deleting one) so that you don't lose any information.

Family Tree Maker can assess your tree and show you individuals who might be duplicates.

Note: Before you merge individuals, make a backup of your tree. If you need help see "Backing Up a Tree File" on page 231.

Finding Duplicate Individuals

After adding a lot of new information or merging a family member's tree with yours, it's a good idea to check for duplicate individuals.

1. Click **Edit>Find Duplicate People**. The Find Duplicate People window opens.

In the Person 1 and Person 2 columns you'll see the individuals who might be duplicates. (You can click a column header to sort a column alphabetically.) In the third column you'll see a match score—the higher the number the more likely the individuals are a match; a 1,000 means the individuals are almost exact matches.

2. To merge a pair of individuals (or just compare the two), click their row in the window and click **Compare/Merge**. The Individual Merge window opens. To complete the merge, continue with step 5 in the next section, "Merging Individuals."

Merging Individuals

If you discover that two individuals in your tree are actually the same person, you can merge the two together and retain all the facts and sources associated with each person.

1. Go to the **Tree** tab on the People workspace and click the name of one of the duplicate individuals in the Index.

2. Click **Person>Merge Two Specific Individuals**. The Index of Individuals window opens.

3. Click the name of the other duplicate individual. You can use the scroll bar to move up and down the list, or you can type a name (last name first) in the **Find** field.

4. Click **OK**. The Individual Merge window opens.

The two columns show the facts attached to each individual. You can decide how the information is merged together and whether you want to keep or discard alternate facts.

5.   Use the buttons next to the facts to determine how each fact will be merged:

  •   To keep a fact and mark it as preferred, select the button next to the fact. The corresponding fact for the other individual will be merged as an alternate fact unless you discard it.

  •   To remove a fact, click the Alternate arrow and choose "Discard" from the drop-down list. Though you may discard any fact you like, it is usually a good idea to keep all facts in case they turn out to be relevant.

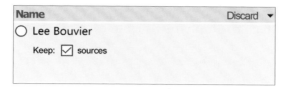

If you discard a fact, you can keep its sources, media, and notes items by selecting the corresponding checkboxes.

Note: To learn more about preferred and alternate facts, see "Adding Alternate Facts" on page 45.

6. Click **OK** to complete the merge.

Removing an Individual from a Tree

If you've mistakenly added an individual who isn't related to you, don't worry, Family Tree Maker makes it easy to delete any individual and his or her information from your tree.

1. Go to the **Tree** tab on the People workspace.

2. Make sure the individual you want to delete is the focus of the Index and family group view.

3. Click **Person>Delete Person**. A message asks you to confirm that you want to delete the individual. Click **Yes**.

All notes, tasks, and media links associated with the person will be permanently deleted.

Note: Whenever you want to remove someone permanently from your tree, always use the Delete Person menu option. If you try to delete someone by removing his or her name from the Name fact, you won't actually delete the individual—or any of his or her facts or relationships.

Removing a Marriage

As you continue your research you might find that you've connected a couple incorrectly. You'll need to delete any marriage facts you've entered and also detach the individuals from each other.

1. Go to the **Tree** tab on the People workspace and select the appropriate couple.

2. Click the **Person** tab for one of the individuals. Right-click the **Marriage** fact and choose **Delete Fact**. A message asks you if you want to delete this fact (and associated notes) from both individuals. Click **Yes**.

    Note: If you don't delete the Marriage fact, the individual will still be considered married but to an unknown person.

3. To detach the individual from the current spouse, click **Person>Attach/Detach Person>Detach Selected Person**. The Detach window opens.

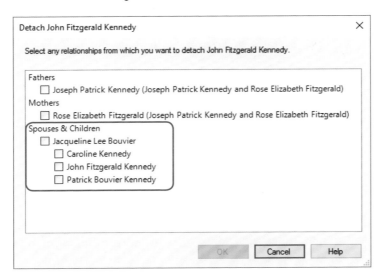

4. Click the checkbox for the incorrect spouse. If the couple has children, you can click their checkboxes to detach them from the selected individual too.

5. Click **OK**.

Detaching a Child from the Wrong Parents

If you've added a child to the wrong parents, you can detach the child from the family without deleting them from your tree.

1. Go to the **Tree** tab on the People workspace.

2. Make sure the correct family is the focus of the family group view. Then click the child's name.

3. Click **Person>Attach/Detach Person>Detach Selected Person**. The Detach window opens.

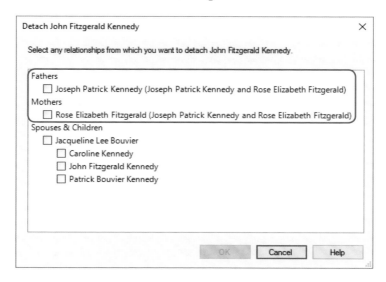

4. Click the checkboxes next to the father and/or mother.

5. Click **OK**.

Attaching a Child to a Father and Mother

If you've added an individual and his or her parents to your tree, but you did not know they were related when you entered them, you can still link them together.

1. Go to the **Tree** tab on the People workspace.

2. Make sure the individual you want to attach to his or her parents is the focus of the Index or family group view.

3. Click **Person>Attach/Detach Person>Attach Mother/Father.** The Select the Mother/Father to Attach window opens.

4. Choose the father or mother from the list and click **OK**. If the father or mother has multiple spouses, you'll need to choose which family the child belongs to.

5. Choose the appropriate family and click **OK**.

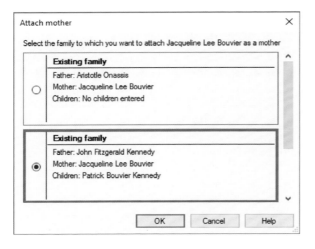

Fixing Text Mistakes

It's easy to introduce errors into your tree. Perhaps you transcribed a record too quickly or imported incorrect notes from a family member's tree. Family Tree Maker has several tools that can help look for misspellings, inaccurate dates, and duplicate facts.

Global Spell Checker

The global spell checker lets you search for errors in your tree.

1. Click **Tools>Global Spell Check**.

2. Change these options as necessary:

    •   **Fact descriptions.** Select this checkbox to check spelling in fact descriptions.

    •   **Media.** Click this checkbox to check spelling in media captions and descriptions.

    •   **Sources.** Click this checkbox to check spelling in citation detail and citation text fields.

    •   **Notes.** Click to check spelling in all notes.

    •   **Tasks.** Click to check spelling in all tasks in the research to-do list.

3. Click **Begin Checking**. If the spell checker finds a potential error, it displays the word in the "Not in dictionary" field.

4. Replace or ignore the word using the spell check buttons. A message tells you when the spell check is complete. Click **OK**.

Find and Replace Tool

You may have mistakenly spelled an individual's name wrong throughout your tree or perhaps you abbreviated a place name that you want to spell out now. You can use Find and Replace to correct these mistakes—one by one or all at the same time.

1. Click **Edit>Find and Replace**. The Find and Replace window opens.

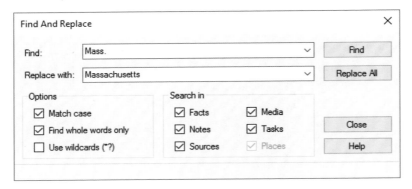

2. Enter the term you want to search for in the **Find** field. Then enter the new term you want to use in the **Replace with** field.

3. Choose one or more of the following:

    •   To find words that match your search exactly (uppercase and lowercase), select the **Match case** checkbox.

    •   To find entire words that match your search, select the **Find whole words only** checkbox. (For example, a search for Will would not show results for William or Willton.)

    •   To search using wildcards, click the **Use wildcards** checkbox. Wildcards allow you to search for one or more missing characters. An asterisk (*) replaces multiple characters; a search for "Mas*" could find Massachusetts, Masonville, or

Masterson. A question mark (?) replaces one character; a search for Su?an would find Susan and Suzan.

4. Click the checkbox for each part of the tree you want to search in. If you're not sure where the information is, you might want to select all of the checkboxes.

5. Click **Find**. The first result that matches your terms appears.

6. If you want to replace the search term with the new term, click **Replace**.

Tip: You can replace all matching search results by clicking the Replace All button. Before you do, back up your tree file because you cannot undo these changes.

7. To find the next match, click **Find Next**.

8. Continue searching and replacing terms as necessary.

Merging Duplicate Facts

If you have multiple versions of the same fact, you can merge them together. You can choose only one date and place for the fact. If you have multiple descriptions, they will be combined into one.

1. Select the appropriate individual and go to the **Person** tab on the People workspace.

2. Click the **Facts** button, right-click one of the duplicate facts, and then select **Merge Duplicate Facts**.

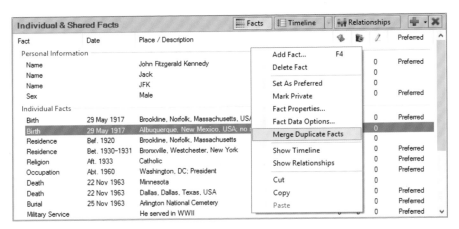

3. The Merge Duplicate Facts window opens.

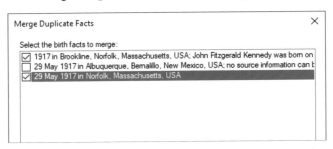

4. Click the checkboxes next to the facts you want to merge and click **Next**.

5. Select the date and location you want to keep.

Merge Duplicate Facts	✕

Select the date to keep:

> May 1917
> 29 May 1917

Select the place to keep:

> Brookline, Norfolk, Massachusetts, USA
> USA

Select the description(s) to keep:

> John Fitzgerald Kennedy was born on 29 May 1917 in Brookline, Norfolk, Massachusetts, U

Any source citations, notes, and/or media items that are not duplicates will be kept.

Back	Finish	Cancel	Help

6. Click **Finish**.

Running the Data Errors Report

Family Tree Maker can search your tree and identify potential errors. For example, it can look for blank fields or date problems, such as an individual being born before his or her parents were born. It's a good idea to run the Data Errors Report (fig. 14-1) periodically to make sure your tree is as error free as possible.

Data Errors Report		
Name	**Birth Date**	**Potential Error**
Bennett, Virginia Joan		The birth date is missing.
Bouvier, Jacqueline Lee	28 Nov 1929	Possible duplicate event Arrival Possible duplicate event Departure
Fitzgerald, Catherine	Abt. 1824	The individual has the same last name as his/her spouse, John Fitzgerald. The marriage date is missing.
Fitzgerald, John	Abt. 1824	The individual has the same last name as his/her spouse, Catherine Fitzgerald. The marriage date is missing.
Fitzgerald, Rose Elizabeth	21 Jul 1890	This individual's children sort order may be incorrect.

Figure 14-1. A Data Errors Report.

1. Go to the **Collection** tab on the Publish workspace. In Publication Types, click **Person Reports**.

2. Double-click the **Data Errors Report** or click the report icon and then click the **Create Report** button or the **Detail** tab.

3. To determine which errors the report lists, click the **Errors to include** button on the editing toolbar. The Errors to Include window opens.

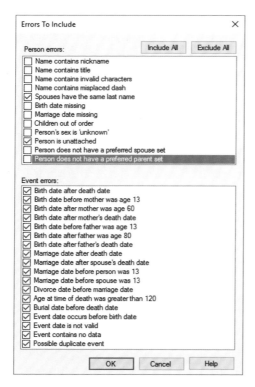

4. Click the checkboxes next to the errors you want to search for. Then click **OK**. The Data Errors Report opens.

5. To fix the error immediately, simply double-click an individual's name in the report. An editing window will open.

Standardizing Locations

When you import a tree or manually enter a location, Family Tree Maker checks the location against its database of three million places. If any misspellings are found, or if the place doesn't match any sites in the database, a location is considered "unrecognized."

You'll want to examine these "unrecognized" locations occasionally and make any necessary changes. In some cases, you may want to leave the name exactly as it is. For example, if a town or city no longer exists, or the county boundaries have changed over the years, it is perhaps most appropriate to keep the location's name as it is. However, in most cases, you'll want to identify locations to keep your tree consistent and to make sure that locations are grouped together correctly on the Places workspace.

Identifying a Single Location

If you see a question mark icon next to a place name in your tree, you can try to identify the place in the locations database.

1.   Click the **Places** button on the main toolbar. Click an unidentified location (with a question mark icon) in the Places panel. On the right side of the window, you'll see the location's name and any people and events associated with it.

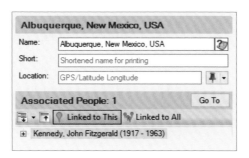

2. Click the question mark icon next to the location's name.

3. Do one of the following:

- If a suggestion matches the location in your tree, click its name in "Suggested place names" and click **Replace**.

- If no locations are a match, you can ignore only part of a location by clicking the **Move first segment to place detail** arrow. When the updated location finally has a match, click **Replace**. (You can also click **Ignore** to leave the location as it is.)

  Note: Ignoring part of a location doesn't change how it is displayed in your tree; it simply allows the location to be grouped together correctly on the Places workspace.

Identifying Multiple Locations

If you've imported a tree or merged someone's tree into your own, you'll likely have many place names that don't match the other locations in your tree. Instead of updating each location one at a time, you can identify multiple locations at once.

1. Click **Tools>Resolve All Place Names**.

2. To back up your tree file before you update your locations, click **Yes**. The Backup window opens. Change any options as necessary and click **OK**.

    The Resolve All Place Names window opens. Each unrecognized location is listed, along with a suggested replacement location.

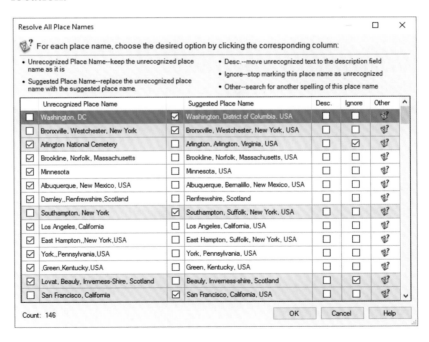

3. For each listed location, click the checkbox for the option you want to use:

- **Unrecognized Place Name.** Click this checkbox to leave the location as it is.

- **Suggested Place Name.** Click this checkbox to change the current location to the suggested location.

- **Desc.** Click this checkbox to move the location's name from the Place field to the Description field.

- **Ignore.** Click this checkbox to leave the location as it is. The location name will no longer be "unrecognized."

- **Other.** To see other locations that might match the current place name, or to ignore only part of a location, click **Other**. The Resolve Place Name window opens. When you identify a matching location, click **Replace**.

4. When you've chosen an option for each location, click **OK**.

Finding Missing Media Items

If you move a media item on your computer after you've added it to a tree, you won't be able to view, print, or export the item until it is relinked to your tree. You can search for missing media items individually or all at once.

Finding a Single Missing Media Item

On the Media workspace, the editing panel shows the media item's name and location on your computer. If a media item is no longer linked to your tree, you'll see a red "File not found" message (fig. 14-2). To relink the media item, click it and locate the item.

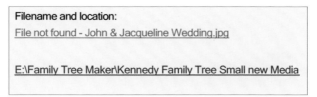

Filename and location:

File not found - John & Jacqueline Wedding.jpg

E:\Family Tree Maker\Kennedy Family Tree Small new Media

Figure 14-2. A missing media file.

Finding All Missing Media Items

Family Tree Maker can search for missing media items and help
you relink them to your tree.

1. Click the **Media** button on the main toolbar. Click **Media>Find
    Missing Media**. A list of unlinked images appears.

2. Click the checkboxes next to the items you want to locate or
    click **Select All** to find all missing media items.

3. Click **Search**. If Family Tree Maker finds the file, its current
    location is displayed in the Path column; a check mark appears
    in the Status column. If Family Tree Maker can't find the file,
    click its row in the Path column to search for it yourself.

4. When you're finished, click **OK**.

Troubleshooting

Although we hope you never have problems while using Family Tree Maker, all computers and software have their own incompatibilities. This chapter identifies several common problems and includes ways to fix them.

If you don't find an answer to your question, you can get help at support.familytreemaker.com. Enter your issue in the search field and press **Enter**.

When dealing with technical issues, you should make sure that your computer meets or exceeds the system requirements. Also, keep in mind that the more information you enter, the greater the amount of free hard drive space and available RAM you will need. If you plan to include many pictures, audio, or video files in your trees, you will need a substantial amount of hard drive space.

Ancestry Issues

Because Family Tree Maker and Ancestry are closely linked together, you may encounter some website-related issues when using Family Tree Maker.

I am having problems logging in to Ancestry.

Your computer may not be connected to the Internet. Make sure that you are able to access and sign in to Ancestry using a normal Web browser (Internet Explorer, etc.). If you are unable to access the website, you'll need to fix your Internet connection first.

Make sure Internet access is enabled in Family Tree Maker. To do this, go to the **File** menu and select **Go Online**. (If the menu item "Go Offline" appears, Internet access is already enabled. To make absolutely sure, you may want to select "Go Offline" and then select the "Go Online" item again.)

Your firewall settings or security software may be preventing Family Tree Maker from connecting to the Ancestry server. You may need to add FTM.exe as an exception to your security software or firewall. For information about changing firewall settings, contact your security software manufacturer directly.

Make sure that your computer's date and time are correctly set to your time zone. They can be adjusted by clicking on the date and time in the lower right-hand corner of your desktop, then selecting "Change date and time settings...".

I have a problem getting Ancestry hints.

Make sure your FTM tree is uploaded and linked to the Ancestry tree.

Click **Tools** > **Options** and make sure the **Show hints from Ancestry** checkbox is selected. To be absolutely certain, you may want to deselect the checkbox and then select it again.

Sign in to Ancestry using a Web browser and make sure there are hints in the Ancestry tree to which your FTM tree is linked. Try closing and then opening your FTM tree.

When I try to access a record on Ancestry, I see an error message. What does it mean?

Occasionally you may come across one of these error messages:

Document contains no data.

503 Service Unavailable.

We're sorry, this page is temporarily unavailable.

These types of errors usually indicate a temporary issue with your Internet Service Provider (ISP) or the Ancestry website. To resolve the issue, refresh or reload the Web page by pressing **CTRL+F5**. Or you can try to view the page again later.

If you keep seeing the same error message, you should clear your temporary Internet files.

I have problems printing and saving information I find on Ancestry when I access the website through Family Tree Maker.

The Web Search feature lets you add records from Ancestry and also navigate the entire website. However, some features on Ancestry work better when accessed through a regular Web browser rather than through the Family Tree Maker browser because of its limited functionality. If you're having trouble using an Ancestry feature in Web Search, click the **Browser Options** button (left of the Address field) and choose "Open in New Window" to open the site in a regular Web browser.

FamilySync Issues

I get an error message when I try to sync my FTM and Ancestry trees.

To improve your chances of trouble-free syncing, read "Best Practices for Syncing" in the FTM Support Center. (Go to support.familytreemaker.com and enter "best practices" in the search field.)

Check your Internet connection. If you have a dial-up Internet connection, or you have disabled your broadband connection, establish your Internet connection before you open Family Tree Maker. Make sure you are able to get to other websites.

Make sure Internet access is enabled in Family Tree Maker. To do this, go to the **File** menu and select **Go Online**. (If the menu item "Go Offline" appears, Internet access is already enabled. To make absolutely sure, you may want to select "Go Offline" and then select the "Go Online" item again.)

Generate and send a Sync Error Report. Sending a Sync Error Report (sometimes also called a "Sync Error Log") will help technical support determine exactly what is causing the issue you are experiencing when using FamilySync. The easiest way to generate and send a Sync Error Report is to use the **FamilySync Report** dialog. This will create a report and deliver it to the Family Tree Maker technical support team automatically. You can access the dialog in two ways:

- If an error occurs during syncing, the **FamilySync Report** dialog will open automatically.

- You can open the dialog at any time by choosing **Send Sync Error Report** from the **Help** menu.

I synced my trees and I can't see all the media items in my Ancestry tree. What happened?

When you synchronize trees, data is transferred immediately. Media items are processed separately in the background. Because of this it may take a while for all your images to appear in your Ancestry tree. You can track the progress of your media sync using the Media processing status bar on the main toolbar.

Relationship Mistakes and Unknown Spouses

You can easily fix an incorrect relationship by detaching an individual, then attaching them to the correct person in your tree. In the case of an unknown spouse, you would detach them from the person in your tree and their children, if any. For help, read "Fixing Relationship Mistakes" in the FTM Support Center. (Go to support.familytreemaker.com and enter "relationship mistakes" in the search field.)

Damaged or Corrupt Files

I don't have a backup of my tree and my file won't open. Is there anything I can do?

Files can be damaged by viruses, a merging of corrupt data, the improper shut down of Family Tree Maker, and more. If you don't have a backup of your tree, you can try to fix your current file. For help, read "Repairing a Tree File" in the FTM Support Center. (Go to support.familytreemaker.com and enter "repair" in the search field.)

Display Problems

In Family Tree Maker buttons and fields overlap each other and are difficult to read. How can I fix this?

Display problems can occur if you have changed the default Windows font size. You'll need to change your Windows font size, or you can drag open a window to enlarge it.

For more information on this issue, read "Fixing Display Issues" in the FTM Support Center. (Go to support.familytreemaker.com and enter "display issues" in the search field.)

Error Messages

You may occasionally receive an error message while installing or using Family Tree Maker. Here are some messages you might see:

Family Tree Maker has encountered a problem and needs to close or Family Tree Maker has stopped working.

Usually this message is caused by an old or corrupt Family Tree Maker configuration file. For instructions on deleting this file, read "Resetting Program Settings" in the FTM Support Center. (Go to support.familytreemaker.com and enter "resetting" in the search field.) If you keep seeing this message, please contact technical support.

You are not connected to the Internet or are behind a firewall.

This message appears when your Internet connection is inactive or when something is blocking Family Tree Maker from using your Internet connection.

You must be logged on as an administrator.

In Windows you may need to run Family Tree Maker as an administrator. To do this, right-click the Family Tree Maker icon and select "Run as Administrator." If you need more help, read "How to Give FTM Administrator Privileges" in the FTM Support Center. (Go to support.familytreemaker.com and enter "admin" in the search field.)

Tree File Importing Errors

I get an error message when I try to import a tree.

It is important to determine if the importing problem is specific to one tree file or to multiple tree files. If you can import some tree files but not others, the tree file may be damaged. You may need to revert to a backup. If you cannot import any tree files, create a new test tree file in Family Tree Maker and export it as a GEDCOM. Now try to import the test tree file. If it doesn't import, you'll need to uninstall and reinstall the software. For more information, read "Uninstalling FTM" and "Manually Uninstalling FTM" in the FTM Support Center. (Go to support.familytreemaker.com and enter "uninstall" in the search field.)

Incorrect tree file version.

This message appears when you're importing a tree file that is not supported by Family Tree Maker (for example, if someone shares a Family Tree Maker tree file with you but you're using a different version of the software). For help importing a tree file, read "Importing an Existing File" in the FTM Support Center.

(Go to support.familytreemaker.com and enter "import existing" in the search field.)

Installation Problems

For the majority of users, Family Tree Maker installs without any problems. However, if you are experiencing difficulties you should test the DVD on another computer to verify that the disc is good. If the installation DVD is damaged, contact technical support for assistance. If the DVD works on another computer, one of these topics may help you resolve the problem.

I can't get Family Tree Maker to install on my computer.

Occasionally Family Tree Maker won't install on your computer because of conflicts with other software, corrupt user profiles, and other reasons. For help troubleshooting this issue, read "Troubleshooting Installation" in the FTM Support Center. (Go to support.familytreemaker.com and enter "installation" in the search field.)

Nothing happens when I put the DVD in the DVD drive.

There may be fingerprints, scratches, or dust on your DVD. Remove the DVD from the drive and gently wipe it with a clean towel. Do not wipe in a circular motion; wipe from the inside edge to the outside edge.

The Windows Autorun feature may be turned off. You'll need to start the installation program yourself. Make sure the DVD is in the DVD drive. Press **Windows logo key + R**.

In the **Open** field, type "d:/setup/setup". (The "d" in "d:/setup" stands for drive D. If you are installing from another drive, type that letter instead. For example, from drive E, type "e:/setup/setup".) Then click **OK**.

I get a message saying there isn't enough hard drive space to install the program.

You may be out of space on the drive where Windows is installed, the drive where you're attempting to save the program, or the drive where your temporary folder is located. To ensure that you have sufficient hard drive space, check the following:

- **Hard drive space available on the drive where Windows is installed.** You need to have at least 900MB of space available on the drive where Windows is installed. In addition, Windows needs at least 15% of the total space on your hard drive to be free to run properly after Family Tree Maker has been installed. You may encounter problems if you have less.

- **Hard drive space available on the drive where Family Tree Maker is saving your trees.** You generally need to have three times the size of your tree file available because of the way many Windows programs (including Family Tree Maker) save files. For example, if your tree file is 400,000 bytes, you actually need 1,200,000 bytes (1.2MB) available to save it.

- **Temporary hard drive space.** Windows has a temporary storage folder, usually C:\Windows\Temp. This folder should be cleaned out on a regular basis. To do this, close all open programs. Press **Windows logo key + R**. Then, in the **Open** field, type "temp" and click **OK**. Windows opens the Temp folder. Make sure the window's title bar says "Temp" and delete any files.

I get a message saying, "You must be logged on as an administrator."

In Windows access to common tasks and programs may be managed by the User Account Control (UAC). If you are trying to access Family Tree Maker as a standard user (meaning without administrative privileges), you won't be able to open the program.

You will need to run Family Tree Maker as an administrator. If you need instructions, read "How to Give FTM Administrator Privileges" in the FTM Support Center. (Go to support. familytreemaker.com and enter "admin" in the search field.)

How do I manually uninstall Family Tree Maker?

If you have uninstalled and reinstalled the Family Tree Maker program and it still opens with the error message, "Program has encountered a problem and must close" (or something similar), you may need to manually remove Family Tree Maker. To troubleshoot this issue, read "Manually Uninstalling FTM" in the FTM Support Center. (Go to support.familytreemaker.com and enter "uninstall" in the search field.)

Internet Connection Problems

I get an error message that says, "You are not connected to the Internet or are behind a firewall."

This error occurs when there is no connection to the Internet, or a firewall is blocking Family Tree Maker from using your Internet connection.

Make sure Internet access is enabled in Family Tree Maker. To do this, go to the **File** menu and select **Go Online**. (If the menu item "Go Offline" appears, Internet access is already enabled. To make absolutely sure, you may want to select "Go Offline" and then select the "Go Online" item again.)

Check your Internet connection. If you have a dial-up Internet connection, or you have disabled your broadband connection, establish your Internet connection before you open Family Tree

Maker. Make sure you are able to get to other websites. If you are still unable to use Family Tree Maker online features, you can troubleshoot this issue. Read "Troubleshooting Connectivity Issues" in the FTM Support Center. (Go to support.familytreemaker.com and enter "connectivity" in the search field.)

PDF Problems

I am unable to save a chart as a PDF.

If you have problems saving reports and charts as PDFs, you may need to designate yourself as an administrator on your computer. If you need instructions, read "How to Give FTM Administrator Privileges" in the FTM Support Center.
(Go to support.familytreemaker.com and enter "admin" in the search field.)

Also, be aware that PDFs in Family Tree Maker are limited to 200 inches by 200 inches. If your chart is larger than this, the contents will be cropped.

Performance Issues

Family Tree Maker is running slowly. What can I do?

If Family Tree Maker is running more slowly than expected, here are a few steps you can take to increase the software's performance.

- Make sure your computer meets or exceeds the system requirements.

- Run the Compact File tool to reindex your file and remove unnecessary data. (For instructions see "Compressing a Tree File" on page 225.)

- Check your tree for duplicate individuals or sources. Merge them as necessary.

- Work offline. Consider temporarily disabling Internet access in Family Tree Maker. To do this, go to the **File** menu and choose **Go Offline**.
- Turn off Ancestry and FamilySearch hints. To do this, go to the **Tools** menu and choose **Options**. Deselect **Show hints from Ancestry** and **Show hints from FamilySearch** and click **OK**.
- Disable Fastfields. Disabling Fastfields in large databases can also speed things up. To do this, go to the **Tools** menu and choose **Options**. Deselect all checkboxes in the **Use fastfields for** section and click **OK**.

Printing Problems

Many printing problems are related to the specific printer you're using. Before you begin, make sure your printer is hooked up correctly, turned on, and connected to the computer. Also, make sure you're familiar with any documentation that came with your printer. If you don't find your issue in the topics below, you may want to contact technical support for the printer's manufacturer.

I am unable to print in Family Tree Maker.

Try to print an image or document from another program. This will verify whether or not the printer is functioning properly. If you can print something using another program, the issue may be a conflict with Family Tree Maker.

The most common cause of printing issues involves conflicts between the program and printer driver, which acts as a translator between the printer and the program. Verify that the driver for your printer is up to date. Most manufacturers offer these drivers as free downloads from their websites.

Your computer may be running low on memory. Family Tree Maker requires that you have at least 2GB of physical memory to run. If you don't have enough memory, Family Tree Maker might take a long time to perform certain tasks like printing, especially if you have a large tree. Try closing other programs to make more memory available. If the performance is still sluggish, you might want to add more memory to your system.

Why is Family Tree Maker printing slowly?

Printing from Windows, especially when printing graphics, can be slow. To improve your printing speed, try printing images at a lower quality. (Although be aware that the final product won't look as nice.)

The Windows spool settings may be slowing down printing. To disable these features, see your Microsoft Windows user's guide. You may also need to refer to the printer's documentation.

My photos are not printing clearly.

Try changing the image to a different format before you import it. Family Tree Maker accepts a variety of common file formats.

The original image may be of poor quality. If you scanned the photograph, you may need to rescan it.

Family Tree Maker crashes when I print charts and reports.

Verify that the driver for your printer is up to date. Most manufacturers offer these drivers as free downloads from their websites.

Program Unexpectedly Shuts Down

Family Tree Maker may shut down unexpectedly, and you may see an error message.

I get a message saying, "Family Tree Maker has stopped working," or "Family Tree Maker has encountered an error and needs to close."
Usually this message is caused by an old or corrupt Family Tree Maker configuration file. For instructions on deleting this file, read "Resetting Program Settings" in the FTM Support Center.

(Go to support.familytreemaker.com and enter "resetting" in the search field.) If you keep seeing this message, please contact technical support.

Family Tree Maker keeps crashing. What can I do?
If Family Tree Maker is crashing frequently it could be due to needed system or program updates, file corruption, or other reasons. For help troubleshooting this issue, read "FTM 2017 Crashes or Closes Unexpectedly" in the FTM Support Center. (Go to support.familytreemaker.com and enter "crashes" in the search field.)

Software Updates

How can I make sure I have the latest software updates?
Periodically, updates that fix bugs and add new features in Family Tree Maker are released. Make sure that Family Tree Maker is up to date by going to the **Help** menu and choosing **Check for Update**.

You may need to run Family Tree Maker as an administrator in order to check for updates. If you need instructions, read "How to Give FTM Administrator Privileges" in the FTM Support Center. (Go to support.familytreemaker.com and enter "admin" in the search field.)

You can also check for free updates at www.familytreemaker.com.

Glossary

Ahnentafel German for ancestor table. In addition to being a chart, it also refers to a genealogical numbering system.

ancestor A person you descend from—parent, grandparent, great-grandparent, etc.

Ancestry Hint The green leaf indicating that a person might have matching records on Ancestry.

Ancestry Member Tree (AMT) Same as Ancestry tree.

Ancestry tree An online family tree you have created on or uploaded to Ancestry.

blended family A family composed of a couple and their children from previous relationships and/or marriages, as well as any children they have together.

combined family view An option in the family group view that lets you view blended families.

CSV Comma Separated Values. A file format that organizes information into fields and can be imported into a spreadsheet.

descendant A person who descends from you—your child, grandchild, great-grandchild, etc.

editing panel   A section of a workspace that lets you easily edit and view information for a specific individual or item.

export   To transfer data from one computer to another or from one computer program to another.

family group sheet   A chart or report that displays information about a single family—father, mother, and children.

family group view   Shows a single family—father, mother, and their children—in Family Tree Maker.

family view   One of the display options for the tree viewer on the People workspace. Similar to the vertical pedigree chart.

FamilySearch hint   The blue square indicating that a person might have matching records on FamilySearch.org.

FamilySync   A feature that lets you link trees from Family Tree Maker and Ancestry so that changes made to an FTM tree will be reflected in the Ancestry tree and vice versa.

Fastfields   A feature that reminds you of locations and people you've entered previously so that when you type a new place or name, you'll see possible matches.

FTM tree   A family tree you have created in or downloaded to Family Tree Maker.

GEDCOM   GEnealogical Data COMmunication. A standard designed by the Family History Department of The Church of Jesus Christ of Latter-day Saints for transferring data between different genealogy software programs.

genealogy report   A narrative-style report that details a family through one or more generations and includes basic facts about each member.

generation   The period of time between the birth of one group of individuals and the next—usually twenty-five to thirty years.

given name   The first (and middle) name given to a child at his or her birth. Also known as a Christian name.

hint   See Ancestry Hint and FamilySearch hint.

home person   The main individual in your tree.

HTML   HyperText Markup Language. The standard language for creating and formatting Web pages.

icon   A small picture or symbol that represents a program, file, or folder on your computer. Double-clicking an icon causes the program to run, the folder to open, or the file to be displayed.

import   To bring a file into a program. The file may have been created in the same or a different program.

maternal ancestor   An ancestor on the mother's side of the family.

paternal ancestor   An ancestor on the father's side of the family.

PDF   Portable Document Format. A file format that retains printer formatting so that when it is opened it looks as it would on the printed page.

pedigree chart   A chart that shows the direct ancestors of an individual. Also known as an ancestor tree.

pedigree view   One of the display options for the tree viewer on the People workspace. Similar to the standard pedigree chart.

preferred   A term Family Tree Maker uses in reference to parents, spouses, or duplicate events indicating that you want to see the preferred selection first or have it displayed in charts and reports.

primary person   The individual who is currently the focus of the workspace, chart, or report.

RTF   Rich Text Format. A basic text file format that can be opened in almost all word-processing programs.

siblings   Children of the same parents.

Smart Stories   A tool that helps you compose stories using facts, sources, notes, and images from your tree.

Soundex   A system that assigns a code to a surname based on how it sounds rather than how it is spelled.

source   A place where you found specific information, such as a historical records, a book, or an interview.

source citation   The individual details about where information is located within a source.

surname   The family name or last name of an individual.

Web clipping   The ability to "clip" text or images from a Web page and add them elsewhere, like to your Family Tree Maker tree.

Web Dashboard   A feature on the Plan workspace that lets you view your Ancestry account and trees.

Web Merge   A feature that lets you take records you've found on Ancestry and FamilySearch and add them to your Family Tree Maker tree.

workspace   A major grouping of Family Tree Maker features. Each workspace can be opened from the main toolbar.

Index

About the Original Author

Tana L. Pedersen

Tana has been writing and editing in the technology industry for more than fifteen years. She has earned several awards for her writing, including the Distinguished Technical Communication award from the Society for Technical Communication. Tana is author of *Beyond the Basics: A Guide for Advanced Users of Family Tree Maker 2012*, five editions of *The Official Guide to Family Tree Maker*, and co-author of *The Official Guide to RootsWeb.com*.